Removing The I From Life

The Dethroning of King Me

By Steve Etner

Learn more about this book
and its author by visiting our website:
www.overboardministries.com

Copyright © 2018 Overboard Ministries
All rights reserved.
ISBN-13: 978-1-943635-20-7

This book is also available as an eBook.
Visit www.overboardministries.com for details.

All Scripture quotations, unless otherwise indicated, are taken from The Holy Bible, English Standard Version (ESV), copyright © 2001 by Crossway, a publishing ministry of Good News Publishers. Used by permission. All rights reserved.

Scripture quotations marked NIV '84 are taken from The Holy Bible, New International Version. Copyright © 1973, 1978, 1984 by International Bible Society. Used by permission of Zondervan Publishing House. All rights reserved.

Scripture quotations marked NKJV are taken from the New King James Version®. Copyright © 1982 by Thomas Nelson. Used by permission. All rights reserved.

Scripture quotations marked (NLT) are taken from the Holy Bible, New Living Translation, copyright ©1996, 2004, 2015 by Tyndale House Foundation. Used by permission of Tyndale House Publishers, Inc., Carol Stream, Illinois 60188. All rights reserved.

Scripture quotations marked KJV are from the KING JAMES VERSION.

Dedication

"Do not withhold good from those to whom it is due, when it is in your power to do it."
Proverbs 3:27

A book dedication is simply a way to bestow a very high honor on a person (or small group of people) the author wants to thank or otherwise spotlight. Although most of you will not know these names, each of them plays a very important role in the forming of this book.

First, I want to dedicate this book to three men who have encouraged me, prayed for me, and helped me form this book into what it is. From the bottom of my heart, thank you Brian Sigman, Patrick Fox, and Dan Wertman. You guys rock!

Second, I dedicate this book to a man who has been not only my mentor, my accountability partner, and my pastor, but has been my friend through thick and thin. He has, is, and always will be a man I love, respect and honor. Thank you, Phil Byars, for speaking (and modeling) Truth into my heart and life.

Finally, I am honored to dedicate this book to my dear wife. Heather Etner is a woman most of you will probably never meet, but you should. Oh, how I wish you would. Why? Because Heather is—to me—the greatest living example of what it means to be selfless.

Please don't think I'm trying to paint a picture of a perfect woman, for that is not Heather. But she has shown me what it truly means to put God first, others second, and King Me always last. I love you, Heather, and am humbled beyond words that you have chosen to love me.

CONTENTS

Dedication		iii
Foreword		vii
Introduction		xi
One:	Why Did I Do That?	1
Two:	This is not My Life	15
Three:	Choosing Your Choices	33
Four:	A Glorious Game Changer	55
Five:	It's All About ME	75
Six:	Unmasked	91
Seven:	Saved to Sit, Soak, and Sour…NOT!	107
Eight:	Time to Eat!	123
Nine:	Deceived, Duped, and Double-Crossed	137
Ten:	Consider the Source	151
Eleven:	The Favor of a Prepared Mind	165
Twelve:	The Spirit Walk	179
About the Author		199
Acknowledgements		200
About Overboard Ministries		201

FOREWORD

The year was 2011. I had just finished writing my first book, and we couldn't find a publisher interested in taking a risk on a new author. The book publishing industry was in a bit of a tailspin, and a significant shift was underway in the centuries-old system of publishing and selling books.

For a while I believed the prospect of publishing my book was coming to an end, when my friend and mentor, Danny Ray, dropped a ridiculous idea onto the table: "You should start your own publishing company," he advised.

I laughed.

A few months later, Overboard Ministries, LLC was born. I published my first book with the idea that maybe I'd find another author out there, somewhere, who also needed help publishing a book. My wife and I had no idea what that one step would mean for us.

The first call I received from another author interested in our services was from a man named Steve Etner. He had recently attended a technology seminar taught by a pastor out of a church in Indiana, and the two of them began a conversation about life and ministry.

Jamie, the man teaching the seminar, learned that Steve had recently completed a book but was looking for a publisher. Jamie and I went to school together and stayed in touch. He knew I had a publishing company. He knew Steve needed a publisher, and so he helped make the connection.

My phone rang at the time Steve and I had scheduled the call and before I answered it, I took a deep breath, said a prayer, and began a wonderful conversation with Steve. We talked about life, ministry, marriage, his journey, my journey, and about his passion to share the message God had placed on his heart. The call lasted nearly an hour, and when we were finished, Overboard Ministries had its first "other" author ready to publish his first book.

Even more importantly, however, I began a friendship with a man who would help influence and shape my life and ministry.

The book you are holding in your hand is Steve's fourth title with Overboard Ministries, and I'm sure he has several more already planned out in his mind. God has given him an incredible platform from which to point others to Christ and the Scriptures, and Steve is using that platform as well as anyone I know.

You see, writing and having one book published is quite a feat, but to do it four times means you have something significant to say, something that other people want and need to hear. Steve has something significant to share, and what he is sharing, God is using to impact lives around the country and around the world!

I've read every one of Steve's books, including this one, multiple times through the publishing process. Steve's books are powerful because he works hard to point people to Jesus, and he does it as someone who has already traveled the road, as well as being someone who is still in the process himself.

Don't get me wrong, he is an expert, but not the kind that sits on the side and points out all your mistakes and errors while gesturing wildly to help you fix them and get back on track. No, he's the kind of expert that has been where you are and is traveling to where you want to go; he's leading from within the pack.

A few months back I had the privilege of shooting a video series with Steve, working side by side with him for 14-hour days over a one-week period. It was an exhausting and exhilarating week, and that time with him confirmed what I already knew to be true. Steve is a man who is putting into practice the things he teaches, who works every day to live out the very truths he promotes.

So as you read this book, know that you are in the capable hands of a man who is not writing about untried theological concepts or unproven practical theories; rather, he is writing out of brokenness and restoration, out of belief and practice, and you would be wise to glean from what he has written.

He is a redeemed husband and father. He is a shepherd of wounded souls. He is a counselor to lost men. He is a practitioner of what he teaches. He is a theologian who rightly divides God's Word. He is a successful author and speaker. I am thankful he made that call back in 2011. Read this book, and I am confident you will be thankful, too.

Blessings,

Joe Castaneda
Author. Publisher. Founder.
Overboard Ministries.

> "I can do all things through him who strengthens me."
> Philippians 4:13

INTRODUCTION

YOU MIGHT WANT TO READ THIS FIRST

"I just don't understand it; why do I keep doing the things I don't want to do? Why do I struggle so much with sin? I want to be godly! I want to be a godly spouse. I want to be a godly parent. I want to be a godly testimony at work. I want my friends to know that I'm a Christian, not just because I say so, but because that's how I'm living my life—like Christ. So why do I keep screwing up?"

Most of us can relate at some level to the paragraph above—because we too have battled with the same issues.
- Why do I continue to do the things I don't want to do?
- Why can't I gain victory over the stupid sin issues in my life?
- Why can't I be consistent in living a life that glorifies God?

❏ Pause for a moment and re-read those three questions. What one-letter word keeps popping up?

IT'S TIME TO STAGE A COUP

God has promised to equip us with everything we need to live a life that honors him.[1] However, if real change is going to happen, the first thing you need to do is stage a coup.[2] You need to change governments—that is, you need a different spiritual leader sitting behind the big desk in the oval office of your heart. You must choose to remove the "I" from life.

This isn't about you. It never was. It never will be. You need to dethrone and depose the reigning King and allow God to sit in your place—His rightful place.[3]

❏ Why is it so important that God is in charge of my life?

❏ Why is it so hard to let God take charge of my life?

Whoever is reigning in your heart will be calling the shots in your life.[4] When King Me is on the throne, you will live for King Me. When God is reigning in your heart, He will reign in your life.

The outer man (your human behavior) will never consistently glorify God until the inner man (your heart, your spiritual being) is truly glorifying Him *every moment* of every day.[5] In Proverbs 4:23 we read, "Keep your heart with all diligence, for out of it spring the issues of life" (NKJV). When you are thinking about King Me, you're going to live for King Me.

In Psalm 51, following his sin of adultery with Bathsheba,[6] we see David asking God to transform him (to change his outward behavior) by giving him a clean and pure heart (to change his inward thinking). Do you see the significance of David's request? He understood that only a clean and pure heart would bring about the desired external changes in his life. He had learned the hard way that King Me did not make a good King David.

> **Key Thought:** *It is impossible to glorify God in your behavior when YOU are in charge of your heart.*

THE BIRTH OF A BIBLE STUDY

I am so excited that you have decided to join me in this study. Together we are going to learn how to remove the "I" from LIFE, and live our lives focused on glorifying God. Together we are going to discover how to kick King Me off the throne of our hearts and allow God to reign supreme instead. We want to discover what God says about King Me, and we need Him to teach us how to dethrone the King and reveal to us how to keep Him on our heart's throne at all times.

❏ Write out Hebrews 4:12.

The foundation of this Bible study is built completely upon the truths of God's Word, the very words that give us *real* life.[7] That's why it's called a "Bible" study. That's why I had you write out Hebrews 4:12 above. In fact, that's why you'll be writing out a lot of verses during the course of this study.

As you work your way through this book, please don't casually skim over God's Word so that you can read my words. Believe me, God's words are far better (and carry a whole lot more power and authority)! So be prepared to invest time in your Bible.

There are many great "Bible studies" out there that teach fantastic principles of godliness. But I've personally discovered that all too often those books are focused more on the author's thoughts than they are on the words of God. The author will speak on great truths and drive home some thoughtful points, but often uses very little Scripture to support them. If that's the kind of study you're looking for, if you are wanting an "easy read," then this may not be the study for you.

As you read God's Word throughout this study, I challenge you to slow down and read at a pace that enables you to absorb the truths and principles God is trying to teach you. Pray over them. Memorize them. Most of all, live by them.[8]

Work your way through this study intentionally. Look up each of the verses yourself, comparing Scripture with Scripture. Answer the questions sprinkled throughout each chapter. Most of all, don't give up. Change doesn't come easily. If it did, we'd all change. However, when real change does come, it's worth it!

So, are you ready to dive in? Are you ready to dethrone and depose the King, and faithfully worship and serve the Creator and Savior of your soul?

Endnotes

1. 2 Peter 1:3
2. Coup (koo): a sudden and usually violent seizure of power from a reigning government.
3. Isaiah 42:8; 48:11
4. Romans 6:16
5. Proverbs 27:19
6. Read 2 Samuel 11
7. John 6:63
8. Psalm 119:9; James 1:22

"For as he thinketh in his heart, so is he."
Proverbs 23:7 (KJV)

ONE: WHY DID I DO THAT?

- ❏ If you could have one thing in life that would make you happy, what would that thing be?

- ❏ Now, why do you want that particular thing? How can that one thing make you truly happy?

- ❏ In the long run, how is that thing you want going to help you glorify God?

- ❏ Write out James 4:1-2.

Our passions, our fleshly desires, are continuously at war within us (don't take my word for it, read Paul's testimony in Romans 7:15-25…seriously, take a moment and read it). We desire, we want, we long for things that we think we "need" because we're convinced that those things will somehow make King Me feel good and happy. Isn't that what life's all about—feeling good about ourselves and being happy? (Hint: the answer is "no!")

In 1 Chronicles 28:9 David says to his son, "And you, my son Solomon, acknowledge the God of your father, and serve him with wholehearted devotion and with a willing mind, for the Lord searches every heart and *understands every motive behind the thoughts*. If you seek him, he will be found by you; but if you forsake him, he will reject you forever" (NIV '84, emphasis mine).

❏ Write out Proverbs 12:2.

What's your motivation? What lies at the heart of all you do? The title of this book isn't just some cute, trite little saying. To become a person who honors God in all you say and do, you must remove the "I" from your life. It's not about you.

Think about that for a moment. Life gets messed up when King Me is sitting on the throne of your heart. Why? Because God created you to glorify Him, to *live for Him*—not for yourself.[1]

> **Key Thought**: *When you're not functioning according to the manufacturer's specs (God's standards), you're not complete; you're not whole; you're missing something vital to life.*

When you open your Bible to the very beginning, the book of Genesis Chapter One, verse one, you are immediately introduced to the Creator of the Universe, the Architect of all time. He is the almighty, most holy God Himself. Although our English translation renders His name simply as "God," it's actually the name Elohim (pronounced El-o-heem)—the Hebrew name for God—and refers to God as being the Supreme One. That is who we are to live for. Every moment of every day we are to

>   Live
>   For
>   Elohim (God).

Look carefully at the acrostic above. That's the way it's *supposed* to be. That's the purpose of your life and mine. We are to always Live-For-Elohim. Live for God!² However, we mess it all up when we put King Me on the throne. When we add "I" to the acrostic, we do spell "LIFE" but we aren't living that *life* the way God intended. When it's all about Me, the acrostic becomes this:

>   Living
>   *Independently*
>   *From*
>   Elohim

Oh, my friend, that's not true life. Living apart from God is the kind of "life" the enemy wants you to experience. Now, let's face it: that kind of life that may give temporary pleasure, short-term happiness, and a false feeling of fulfillment—but it's not genuine LiFE the way God intended.

> **Key Thought:** *When God is reigning supreme on the throne of your heart, that is when you will experience real life at its fullest, because that's when you will be living the way your Creator intended you to live.*

Carefully consider this: I do what I do because in my heart I want what I want. Now, re-read that.

- ❏ Why is that such a bad thing? Why is it so wrong to have King Me sitting on the throne of my heart?

- ❏ When King Me is sitting on the throne of my heart, I will always worship King me. Why?

- ❏ When King Me is sitting on the throne of my heart, I will expect *everyone* and *everything* else to worship King Me. Why?

- ❏ When King Me is sitting on the throne of my heart, I will expect God to worship King Me. Why?

If I am going to live the life God has called me to live, I must understand that this life isn't about me. It's not about you. Neither of us reigns at the center of the universe. Thank God for that! And yet, all too often we are under the false impression that we do. We think that our primary objective, our purpose of existence, is to enjoy life, to be happy, to experience satisfaction and fulfillment.

When bad things happen, when circumstances or people interfere with our happiness, our world suddenly comes crashing down around us and we are desperate to put it all back together.

Now don't misunderstand me here. I'm not saying that it's wrong to enjoy life, be happy, and experience satisfaction. I am saying *that* should not be your ultimate goal. That is not the purpose or end product. I am also saying that when you make life all about God, that's when you will truly enjoy life. That's when you will experience true happiness, fulfillment and satisfaction!

To be a real, genuine, honest-to-goodness servant of God you must first dethrone and depose King Me. You must remove the "I" from your LIFE. You must learn to *Live For Elohim*. Only then will you be able to be all that you can be. Only then will you truly glorify God.

BATTLE TACTICS 101

In Ephesians 6:12 Paul points out the fact that we are wrestling against "the cosmic powers over this present darkness, against the spiritual forces of evil in the heavenly places." In short, we are engaged in a spiritual battle with a very powerful, very ancient, and very evil foe—none other than the Devil himself. Listen, my friend: your #1 enemy, the Devil, prowls around like a lion looking for someone to devour,[3] and his eyes are fixed on you! But why?

God wants you to glorify Him; Satan does not. Satan isn't necessarily wanting you to bow down and worship him (although I'm pretty sure he'd welcome that), he just doesn't want you to worship God. He doesn't want God to receive any of the glory, so he's going to pull out all the stops to make sure you don't give it to Him.

But he is coy—oh, boy, is he subtle, crafty, and devious. Very rarely will he use a frontal assault. That's too obvious, too blatant and in-your-face. He knows that you'll defend yourself from such an attack. No, he uses guerilla warfare. He deploys his little minions with instructions to play around with your mind. He encourages you to make the choice all on your little lonesome to serve King Me.
- ❏ Write Genesis 4:7.

Now that you've written out the verse, read it again. Every moment of every day, you have choices to make. Do you listen to King Me and do what you want to do, or do you dethrone the King and live in obedience to your Heavenly Father? "If you do what is right," God stands ready to bless you. However, "If you do not do what is right, sin is crouching at your door; it desires to have you." The choice is yours. The choice is *always* yours. What choices are you making?

What a powerful picture God creates here in Genesis 4:7—sin is like a beast crouching at your door. Peter tells us the Devil is like a lion.

That lion is hunkered down in the tall grass just outside the door of your heart. Every muscle is taut with anticipation, ready to pounce the moment you choose to ignore God. Its blood-red eyes are reduced to mere slits as it stares at you. Its hot breath steams out of its nostrils, its fangs dripping acid, eerily hissing as it hits the ground. It desires to have you. It is patiently sitting there, waiting for you to act in a way that honors King Me instead of God. As soon as you do ... BAM!

Never forget, Satan is an old pro at this. He knows what he's doing—but so do we. "We are not unaware of his schemes."[4] Here are just a few of the evil, guerilla-warfare tactics he likes to use on us:

- ❏ Evil Tactic #1: He makes the sinful world system you live in seem desirable. Many people who profess Christ as their Savior begin their Christian life desiring God. They are all gung-ho for Christ. To look at them, you'd say they were "on fire for God." Soon afterward, in steps the enemy who tempts them to focus on worldly things. Those things that the world provides become more attractive and desirable than all that Christ has to offer. Slowly, almost imperceptibly, King Me crawls up onto the throne and takes over.[5]
    - o Why does the world sometimes become more attractive to us than God?

- ❏ Evil Tactic #2: He plays on your self-preservation instincts by tempting you to fear the consequences of a life centered on God. He wants you to worry about the high cost of obedience. He tries to convince you that God wants you to suffer. "If I surrender it *all* to God, I'll have nothing left, and my life won't be worth living!" Satan wants you to believe that God's definition of "blessings" is not really a blessing at all.
    - o What happens when you believe Satan's lie that God's "blessings" aren't worth it?

- ❏ Evil Tactic #3: He tries to convince you to focus on what a great burden it is to live for Christ. It's too hard to pray; it's too difficult to spend quality time with the Lord; it's too challenging to study the Bible every day, and it's nearly impossible to memorize Scripture. The result is a lackluster attempt to be godly that eventually leads you to just give up trying.
  - ○ Why do we struggle with Bible Study and prayer?

- ❏ Evil Tactic #4: He points out that those who are the most dedicated and committed to God are also the ones struggling the most. He whispers in your ear that if you give your life completely over to God, He's going to take away your house, your car, your cushy job, your health, and even your bank account. What kind of a God is that?
  - ○ Why do we worry so much about what God "might do" with *our* possessions if we choose to fully live for Him?

- ❏ Evil Tactic #5: Every time you try to focus on worshiping God with your life, Satan fills your mind with all kinds of distractions.[6] He brings in everyday things to convince you that you have no time, and thus no desire to read your Bible or pray. "I'll do that boring stuff later."
  - ○ When we say, "I want to read my Bible and pray, I want to serve Christ, *but I just don't have the time,*" what is it we're really saying?

- ❏ Evil Tactic #6: He strongly encourages you to rest on your past achievements. He reminds you how enthusiastic you were for God just last month. He points out to you just how much time you've sacrificed for God, how into Bible study you were, and all that you've done in the church. At the same time, he convinces you that you've earned the right to coast—to sit back and take a break, "Just for a little while. After all, I've done my time ... it's someone else's turn."

- ○ What's wrong with that kind of mindset?

In every tactic mentioned above, can you see where King Me is sitting on the throne? Whether you realize it or not, this conflict isn't just happening in the unknown realms around you. This isn't Angels vs. Demons. This isn't the host of Heaven battling against the forces of evil over the final destination of your soul. This is spiritual warfare, my friend, and it's happening in the living room of your heart.

This battle isn't being fought only by your pastor, the elders or deacons of your church, and other "deeply spiritual saints." You are not an innocent bystander, experiencing the unfortunate side effects of someone else's war. You are on the front lines. The enemy is engaging you. You cannot "sit this one out!"

So What's Really Going On?

As a born-again child of God, your soul is secured in God's grace, mercy, love, and forgiveness. Satan can't have you, and he knows that.[7] So why is he bombarding you with his fiery arrows? Why doesn't he just give up and go attack someone else? Why are you a threat to him at all?

- ❏ Why is it so important to Satan that you keep the "I" in your life? Why does he want you to make life all about King Me?

Watch this: Getting you is not his endgame. That's not his goal. He's not trying to take *you* down because he sees you as a great threat to his plan of world-domination. If you're a born-again believer, Satan knows you're a child of God, and that God will never let him have you. But that is exactly why he is hitting you with everything he's got. Confused? Hear me out.

- Who does Satan hate more than anyone or anything else in the universe? Hint: it's not you. Answer: _____
- Who does Satan want to hurt more than anyone else? Hint: it's not you. Answer: _____
- Satan has had it out for God since the very beginning.[8]
- Satan knows that God loves *you*—you are the apple of His eye—God would do anything for you. (In fact, He has! Take a few moments and read the following verses: Isaiah 41:10; Romans 5:8; John 3:16; Romans 8:35-39; 1 John 4:10, 16 and 19).
  - After reading the verses above, write out your response to them.

- So, it stands to reason that if God loves you that much, and Satan wants to hurt God so deeply—what better way to do that, than to attack the love of God's heart—you? Satan wants to hurt God by hurting you.

Now consider this: The Devil is blitzing you with everything he's got, not to attack your soul but to defeat your mind. Satan knows that if he can impress your thinking, he'll impact your living. He knows that what you think will influence what you do.

> **Key Thought:** *If Satan can compel you to live for King Me, you won't be able to serve King Jesus.*

❏ In the space below, write out 2 Corinthians 11:3.

❏ What was Paul afraid of?

❏ Why do you think that was such a concern to Paul?

❏ How should you respond to this truth?

A MATTER OF THE MIND OVER MATTER
I know you've already read this statement a couple of times, but I firmly believe it bears repeating: We do what we do because in our hearts we want what we want.

At the root of all our sinful behavior is wrong thinking. Read the question below, then take a moment and search your heart before you answer.

❏ When you sin, why are you sinning? What's going on in your mind at that moment? How is your mind reasoning or excusing your sinful choices? Why are you doing what you're doing? Why are you saying what you're saying? Why did you make that particular decision when you knew it was wrong? Why?

No matter what sin issue you may be struggling with, at the heart of it all you'll find King Me. When King Me is sitting on the throne of your heart, you're worshipping the wrong god.

- You battle with anger because you are worshipping the wrong god.

- You struggle with lust because you are worshipping the wrong god.
- You are overcome by worry because you are worshipping the wrong god.
- You have a problem with gluttony because you are worshipping the wrong god.
- You covet and steal because you are worshipping the wrong god.
- You (<u>*fill in the blank with whatever sin you're facing*</u>) because you are worshipping the wrong god.

That false god you're worshipping isn't anger, it isn't lust, or worry, or gluttony, or any of a ton of other things. Those are just the byproduct of your worship disorder. The false god you're worshipping is none other than King Me. When King me is on the throne of your heart, you will worship King me.

> **Key Thought:** *King Me is not now, nor ever will be, God.*

"Seriously?" you ask. "The King Me thing, again?" Yup! Get used to it, my friend; you'll be reading about the King a lot in this book, because the King is at the core of all your problems. That is why you need to remove the "I" from LIFE!

The heart of it all is your mind. Proverbs 23:7 says of mankind, "As he thinketh in his heart, so is he" (KJV). In Proverbs 4:23 we read, "Above all else, guard your heart, for it is the wellspring of life" (NIV '84). In both verses, the word "heart" is used in a way that refers to the place where thinking and decision-making occur. Where is that? It's your mind.

❑ Did you notice God's use of the words "above all else" in Proverbs 4:23? What do those words indicate to you?

What you think becomes what you do. That's why God says, above all else—nothing, *absolutely nothing* is more important than this—

guard your mind, because out of it (out of your thinking) comes your behavior (your doing). So, when you change your thinking (your heart) to be godly thinking, you will begin to change your living (your behavior) to be godly living.

- ❏ Imagine for a moment that you are deep in enemy territory. It's late at night and you're exhausted. A guard has been set just outside your tent. What characteristics and qualities of that guard would give you enough confidence to put head to pillow and actually sleep? What are the characteristics and qualities of a "good guard"?

- ❏ Now take that list and answer this: how can you apply those qualities to Proverbs 4:23?

Give It Some Thought

- ❏ This was a powerful first chapter. Take a moment here and write down your thoughts—what stood out to you and what are you going to do about it?

Endnotes

1. See 1 Peter 4:11; 1 Corinthians 6:20; 10:31; Ephesians 3:21; Colossians 3:17; 1 Timothy 1:17
2. 2 Corinthians 5:15; Matthew 6:24, 33; 22:37; Colossians 3:23; Exodus 20:3
3. 1 Peter 5:8
4. 2 Corinthians 2:11 (NIV '84)
5. Matthew 13:20-21
6. 2 Corinthians 11:3
7. See John 3:16; 10:28-29; 1 John 5:13; Romans 5:1; Ephesians 1:13-14
8. See Isaiah 14:12-14; Ezekiel 28:12-18

> "So whether you eat or drink or whatever you do,
> do it all for the glory of God."
> 1 Corinthians 10:31

Two: This is Not *My* Life

Before you go any further in this chapter, read the following verses. (Be sure to invest the time here to look up all the passages of Scripture—this is important.)
- Read 1 Corinthians 10:31 and Colossians 3:17; then compare those verses with Romans 12:2, Matthew 5:13-16, 6:33, and Mark 12:30-31.

Now, based on the verses above, take the time to carefully, thoughtfully, and honestly answer this question:
- ❑ What is the purpose of *your* life—why are *you* alive today?

The fact is, as a child of God, the life you're living is not *your* life. This isn't about you. Contrary to popular opinion, you aren't here on this planet for your own personal pleasure and satisfaction. God gifted you with life so that you could live it for Him and for His glory.[1] All of it. Every bit of it. All the time.
- ❑ So—be honest now—how are you doing with that?

Consider Mitchell. As the son of a pastor, Mitchell had a solid upbringing. Every time the doors of the church were open, Mitchell's family was there. As a teen he was heavily involved in the youth group. He even went to a Christian high school and was active in missions. After graduating, he went to a Bible College, where he immediately connected with a traveling ministry helping churches minister to the children of their congregation.

While in college, Mitchell met a wonderful Christian gal named Lee, and a few months later they were married. By the time Mitchell was 32 years old, he had four wonderful children and was enjoying a successful career in sales. Everywhere Mitchell went, people loved him. He read his Bible daily, attended church weekly, and prayed as often as he could.

However, Mitchell wasn't a happy man. All the money he had saved wasn't bringing the satisfaction he so desperately wanted. All the "friends" he surrounded himself with weren't bringing him happiness. He even tried some of the more "forbidden pleasures" this world had to offer—but it didn't ease his sense that something significant was still missing. In short, King Me wanted more.

As a result, his marriage was falling apart, his family was disintegrating before his eyes, and he began hopping from job to job, always blaming management for his failures and frustrations. Mitchell began to feed an addiction to pornography as an escape mechanism to help him cope with his pain. Of course, this drove him further into depression, anxiety, and despair. King Me was not a happy camper. Finally, Mitchell made a failed attempt at suicide.

Mitchell's story is described well by David in Psalm 39:6. "Man is a mere phantom as he goes to and fro: He bustles about, but only in vain; he heaps up wealth, not knowing who will get it" (NIV '84).

David's son, Solomon, put it this way: "I have seen all the things that are done under the sun; all of them are meaningless, a chasing after the wind" (Ecclesiastes 1:14 NIV '84). He also wrote in Ecclesiastes 2:11, "When I surveyed all that my hands had done and what I had toiled to achieve, everything was meaningless, a chasing after the wind; nothing was gained under the sun." Have you ever felt that way? Have you ever wondered, at the end of the day, "What's the point?"

The problem Mitchell struggled with is one we all can relate to. You see, at the heart of all of Mitchell's problems, failures, and frustrations was a worship disorder. He had turned his focus inward. King Me was sitting high and mighty on the throne of his heart.

READY - SET- GOD!

Mitchell could have saved himself a lot of heartache and frustration if he had only started his quest with God instead of self. Could it be there's a lesson here for us to learn as well? We could save ourselves that same heartache and frustration if we would just start every day with God instead of King Me.

God created you with a purpose. You were designed by the Almighty to glorify Him. It's programmed within your very DNA! It's at the very heart of who you are. God wants you to grow into a deeper relationship with Him. He is calling you to live a godly life that brings honor and glory to Him in *everything* you think, say, and do.[3]

> **Key Thought:** *Whatever you do, whenever you do it, wherever you are as you're doing it, you are to always do it in Jesus' name*[4] *and always for his glory.*[5]
> *Never for King Me.*

❑ Why do *you* worship God?

❑ If God chose to not give you another blessing for the rest of your life, would you still worship Him?

❏ Stop for a moment and take a personal inventory. Look at your life, consider your daily routine, and think about the choices you are making and the things you are doing every day. Are you doing what God created you to do? Are you fulfilling your purpose in life?

True purpose and meaning to life cannot be found in fame or fortune, people or pleasures. All those things are naturally focused on self. Typically, the primary reason we pursue them is to make King Me happy and content. When they fail to achieve that goal—and fail they will, because King Me can never be truly happy—we abandon them for something else in hopes that maybe the next great thing will bring the elusive happiness we so desperately seek.

❏ Isaiah asks a very important question that we would do well to consider. "Why spend your labor on what does not satisfy?"[6] What do you think: why do we waste our time and energy on those things that can't (and won't) bring lasting satisfaction?

Remember our story about Mitchell? Today Mitchell and Lee enjoy a fantastic marriage. They are involved in a counseling ministry through their church, helping couples find hope, healing, and restoration in their marriages, and Mitchell is in full-time ministry.

What happened? What changed? Why the huge turn-around? God showed Mitchell who was sitting on the throne of his heart—and it wasn't God. The Holy Spirit convicted Mitchell of his worship disorder. You see, Mitchell had started with self and ended with God. May I suggest that we learn from his mistake? Remove King Me from the equation altogether and start with God. I don't want to see you reach the end of your life and say, "I have labored to no purpose; I have spent my strength in vain and for nothing."[7]

This is not *My* Life

> **Key Thought:** *"You can't go back and change the beginning, but you can start where you are and change the ending."*[8]

BLOOD, SWEAT AND YEARS

In our household, we like watching the Olympics. Whether it's the Summer or Winter Olympics, it really doesn't matter as long as we can watch those athletes compete. I enjoy seeing the competitors doing things that I could only dream of doing. I can only imagine what it would be like to glide effortlessly across the ice or soar through the air after zipping down an ice-covered hill at break-neck speeds.

I guarantee you that not one of those athletes who stand on the winner's podium, no matter their sport or discipline, age, gender, or country of origin, woke up one day and said on a whim, *"Hey, I wanna go compete in the Olympics!"* They didn't suddenly contact the airlines, buy a plane ticket, hop the next jet over to the Olympic venue, and stand in line to compete.

Before they ever placed a foot on those starting blocks, before they ever stepped up on to the spring board to swim the 100 meters, before they ever flew over the uneven bars, and before they ever did a triple lutz or a quad, they began their journey to the Olympics with an intensive, intentional training program. They shed blood, they sweat buckets, and it took them years to achieve their goal.

In the same way, we are to train ourselves to be godly. To do so, we need to do more than just occasionally read our Bible; more than just go to church every Sunday, singing the songs, putting our tithe in the offering plate, and listening to a good sermon. We need to daily …
- exercise our faith,[9]
- wear our spiritual armor,[10]
- maintain a humble spirit,[11]
- keep our heart pure,[12]
- focus our hope in Christ,[13]

- live in contentment and the fear of God,[14]
- pursue hard after righteousness,[15]
- be patient in trials,[16]
- manifest a gentle spirit,[17]
- and walk in integrity and truth.[18]

Feeling a bit overwhelmed at the moment? That's quite a list, and it's not even a complete one. I don't know about you, but I can feel exhausted just thinking about having to do or be all those things. In fact, if I'm not careful I could easily become discouraged, thinking there's no way on God's green earth that I could ever fulfill that list for even one day, let alone the rest of my life!

The exciting thing is, I don't have to try to manufacture all the things needed to be godly. Why? Because God has already provided them—all of them!

I'VE GOT THE POWER

"(God's) divine power has given us everything we need for life and godliness through our knowledge of him who called us by his own glory and goodness." (2 Pet. 1:3 NIV '84)

Now there's a promise with a punch! God has already given you *everything* you need to live a godly life.

This is so powerful that I've got to repeat that: God has already given you all you need to live a godly life that daily honors and glorifies Him. You've got the power!

What an amazing power it is, too. I want you to notice in 2 Peter 1:3 that it is God's *divine power* that provides us with everything we need to live a godly life. Whose power? Certainly not your power, or mine. It's God's power. It belongs, not to King Me, but to the King of Glory. "Who is this King of glory? (He's) the Lord *strong and mighty*, the Lord *mighty* in battle."[19]

God has given you His power to be godly. So that begs the question, what kind of power does God have?

- It's the power to create the entire universe and all that's in it out of absolutely nothing.[20] Can you do that? Do you have that kind of power?
- "He determines the number of the stars and calls them each by name. Great is our Lord and mighty in power."[21]
- God says, "I form the light and create darkness, I bring prosperity and create disaster; I, the Lord, do all these things."[22] I know I can't do them; can you?
- Jeremiah describes it this way: "God made the earth by his power; he founded the world by his wisdom and stretched out the heavens by his understanding."[23]

Think about it—God simply spoke, and it happened. He said a word, and something came out of nothing. Now that's power! 2 Peter 1:3 is telling us it is that very power that provides us with everything we need to live a godly life. There is absolutely nothing that kind of power cannot do.

Not only is God so powerful that He created the universe out of nothing, Paul tells us that "by his power God raised the Lord from the dead, and he will raise us also."[24] Yes, you read that right. "God raised (Christ) from the dead, freeing him from the agony of death, because it was impossible for death to keep its hold on him."[25] Now that is incomprehensible power. That is the divine power that God has given you to remove the "I" from life and live entirely for God.

Are you able to create something out of nothing? Can you just speak a word and have something appear? Can you stand over the coffin of a loved one, call her by name, and make her rise from the dead? Can you walk on water? Can you talk to a hurricane and make it instantly disappear? Of course not. But God can, and God did![26] God has given you His divine power. God has equipped you with everything you need to honor and glorify Him.

So please don't sit there, whining and whimpering that you can't be consistently godly—yes, you can! You've got the divine power of the almighty, most sovereign God of the Universe within you! Stop trying on your own and start trusting in God.

❑ What are some ways you've tried to be godly in your own power?

> **Key Thought:** *Through Christ you have the ability to consistently, daily, moment-by-moment be the godly person God has called you to be.*

❑ Write out your response to the above statement.

To be perfectly honest with you, right now this is so overwhelming to me that I need to pause for a moment and pray. I ask that you join with me, right here, right now. I want us to pray the words of the Apostle Paul from Ephesians 1:17-22.

"Father, as we are trying to comprehend this truth, please give us the Spirit of wisdom and revelation, so that we may know you better. I pray that the eyes of our hearts may be enlightened so that we can truly know the hope to which you have called us, and the magnificent riches of our inheritance through you.

"Please help us to grasp even a fraction of your supremely great power that you have given to those who believe. That power is *your* mighty strength working inside us. It's the same power you used when you raised Christ from the dead and seated him at your right hand in Heaven.

"Father, you and you alone are far above all rulers and authorities, powers and dominions, and every title that can possibly be given to man. Everything and everyone is under your feet. You are the head over it all. You are head over me, and I gratefully, humbly, completely yield myself to you. Amen."

ABSOLUTELY AWESOME!

When contemplating all that God is, the author of 1 Chronicles writes, "Yours, O Lord, is the greatness and the power and the glory and the majesty and the splendor, for everything in heaven and earth is yours. Yours, O Lord, is the kingdom; you are exalted as head over all. Wealth and honor come from you; you are the ruler of all things. *In your hands are strength and power to exalt and give strength to all.*"[27] Truly, "He rules forever by his power."[28]

It would be very wise for us to follow our Heavenly Father's advice to "be still, and know that (He is) God."[29]

> "Do you not know? Have you not heard? The Lord is the everlasting God, the Creator of the ends of the earth. He will not grow tired or weary, and his understanding no one can fathom. He gives strength to the weary and increases the power of the weak." (Isaiah 40:28-29)

Only "the God of peace, who…brought back from the dead our Lord Jesus, that great Shepherd of the sheep"—*only God*—can "equip you with everything good for doing his will."[30] How awesome is that?

PLUG IT IN, PLUG IT IN

Let me take you back to 2 Peter 1:3 again. You see, Peter specifically points out that this power God has given to us is His "divine" power. That is significant. Peter is telling us that the capability of being godly belongs to God alone.

- ❑ What does it mean to "be godly?" What does a godly person look like?

❏ Write out Ephesians 5:1.

o What is an imitator?

o How do I imitate God?

Key Thought: *Only God can always be godly.*

Now I realize that statement is about as basically fundamental as saying that apples grow on trees and water is wet, but let's take a moment to really think about this.

The ability to consistently live a godly life does not naturally reside within you, nor does it naturally reside within me. On our own we can never be godly—all we can be are people trying to be godly.[31] Only God is godly. This is why, when King Me is sitting on the throne of your heart, you will always fail to live a life that glorifies God.

❏ King Me isn't godly. Why not?

Think for a moment about a cordless power drill without its battery pack. On its own it's a worthless collection of parts that can do nothing. When I pick it up and pull the trigger, nothing is going to happen. It is incapable of doing what it was created to do. Why? Without the battery plugged in, it has no power.

> **Key Thought:** *Just like a power drill without its battery, on our own we're merely a shell, unable to accomplish anything good for God.*

Godliness is NOT you or me intentionally doing or being something. We are not godly people simply because we teach a Sunday School class or serve on this committee or that board at church or lead a small group Bible Study (or even author a book on the topic). You are godly when you allow the Father to live *His natural godliness* through you moment by moment, day by day.

John wrote that for God to become greater in our lives, we must first become less.[32] We must remove the "I" from life. Only when King Me steps off the throne of my heart and I let God take His rightful place will His divine power flow through me, giving me everything I need to live a consistent, godly life.

ALL MEANS WHAT?

Okay, there's one more thing I want you to notice about 2 Peter 1:3. God's divine power has already given you *everything* you need. I love that word "everything." It's literally the word "all." Have you ever stopped to consider what that simple little word actually means?

> **Key Thought:** *"All" means all, and that's all "all" means!*

It is a powerful little word that refers to each and every part of the whole, leaving absolutely nothing out. Think once again about that power drill. As you hold that drill in your hand, the word "all" certainly refers to the unit as a whole; but it also refers to every gear, every tooth in that gear, every wire, every connection, every screw. Each and every part that makes up the whole. Everything.

God's divine power has given you *all* you need for a godly life. That's fantastic! You cannot manufacture godliness on your own, but you don't need to. As a born-again believer, you have God living in you. That means you already have His godliness. All of it! You don't have to go looking anywhere else for it. Only God can be godly, and He has already placed all His godliness within you. You have the power, because you have the all-powerful God within!

I KNOW WHAT I KNOW, DON'T YA KNOW?
So how exactly do we "plug in" to this power to live a godly life? How do we surrender ourselves to the Almighty, and allow Him to live *His* godliness through us? Peter answers that for us in 2 Peter 1:3. He states that we can find everything we need to be godly "through our knowledge of Him who called us by His own glory and goodness."

I want you to catch the fact that it is *through* our knowledge of God that we receive the power to be godly. But what does that mean? First, the word "through" carries with it the idea that this is the instrument or way that something is going to be accomplished. It is *through* your knowledge of God, by means of your knowledge of God, as you grow in your knowledge of God, that you will discover everything you need to live a godly life.

Second, it is important that we pause long enough to make sure we understand the kind of "knowledge" Peter is talking about. If we're not careful we run the risk of misinterpreting this text, and that could be dangerous. You see, when Peter says that our knowledge of God equips us for living a godly life, he's referring to far more than just being able to recite a bunch of facts and figures regarding God. *Knowing* God is far more than just knowing *about* Him.

Facts and figures about God are good; but knowing details about the Creator of the universe isn't necessarily going to help you live a godly life. If all you have is an intellectual understanding of God, the only thing you will have gained is a fair amount of head knowledge (and the awesome ability to win hands-down at Bible trivia games). The Bible warns us that kind of knowledge "puffs up."[33] It makes King Me feel very good.

Peter is telling us that we need to get to know God much deeper than a list of facts and figures. We need to know Him personally.

- ❏ How can a person (how can you) get to know the Creator of the Universe on a personal level?

When your emphasis is simply on increasing your head knowledge of the Bible, you run the high risk of focusing your life around works instead of a relationship. You will see the Christian life as more of a checklist (do this and don't do that) instead of a relationship with your Heavenly Father. You will find it to be more of a burden instead of a blessing, a hassle instead of a help.

As long as we have a checklist approach to Christianity, we will be focused on the "do's and don'ts" of Scripture. We will put all of our attention on right behavior (external action) instead of getting to know the God who gave us those standards (internal relationship).

The result of such a works-oriented "faith" is a strong sense of shame, guilt, and failure every time we mess up. That's not the kind of life God wants you to live. He doesn't want you to "do this" and "stop doing that." That's not what brings Him honor—it's your heart, it's your attitude, it's whom you allow to sit on the throne.[34]

It's only as we truly get to know God on an intimate level that we will learn to trust Him with more and more control over our life. Only when I surrender myself, removing the "I" from life, and yielding *all* of my life over to God, will I become a godly person. That is when King Me gets out of the way and allows God to live out His godliness through me. The result is that I am finally doing godly "things" out of a heart's desire to please God, rather than a sense of Christian duty or a selfish desire to be recognized.

> **Key Thought:** *My behavior will be godly when my heart is godly.*

IT'S ALL IN WHO YOU KNOW (NOT WHAT YOU KNOW)

Unfortunately, some people define godliness as being full of the correct Biblical information. They believe that if they read enough books, attend enough Christian seminars, study as many facts of the Bible as they can, and accumulate enough data about God, then godliness will somehow automatically follow.

Let me be quick to point out that each of these activities has value. There are some great books by Christian authors worthy of reading, and there are wonderful Christian seminars on growing in your relationship with God that are worthy of attending. Reading God's Word is always beneficial.[35]

In fact, any time you are pursuing knowledge of the Bible and how to live the Christian life you are choosing well.

However, Scripture warns that there are also those who "are always learning but never able to come to acknowledge the truth."[36] Oh, my friend, don't become one of those people. It's possible to know the Word of God frontward and backward. However, if that head knowledge is not accompanied by a *change in your life* in response to what you've learned about God, that knowledge is worthless. Beware of becoming so dependent on knowing about Scripture that you never work on applying to your life the things that you already know from Scripture. James warns, "Do not merely listen to the word, and so deceive yourselves. Do what it says."[37]

❑ What's the difference between head knowledge and heart knowledge?

Jesus said to the religious leaders of the day, "You diligently study the Scriptures because you think that by them you possess eternal life. These are the Scriptures that testify about me, yet you refuse to come to me to have life."[38] At first glance it may appear that Jesus is complimenting these guys for being in the Word. But a closer examination reveals something completely different.

Of course they were intent on learning and knowing Scriptures; they were the spiritual leaders of the day—it was expected of them. But their hearts' motivation was wrong. Their focus was on gaining knowledge of the Word of God for the sake of knowledge itself. It was all about King Me sitting on the throne, appearing to be wise and holy in the eyes of the people—not about growing in a deeper relationship with God.

They were placing their hope for eternity upon how much of the Scriptures they knew and "understood." However, they put so much value on their head knowledge that they totally missed the Son of God—the one whom the Scripture is about—who was standing right before them. Jesus verbally grabbed them by the collars of their sanctimonious robes and said, "These are the Scriptures that testify about *Me*!"

Do you have a head knowledge of the Word of God, but not a heart relationship with the God of The Word? You can know great Biblical truths and principles, have passages memorized and know Bible doctrine, but if you are not living out those truths in your daily life, you are not glorifying God. If you are not *living* by the doctrine you know to be true, you are not godly. Period. King Me is sitting on the throne.

IT'S IN THE BOOK
The more time you invest with your Heavenly Father, the more you get to truly know Him. The more you know Him, the greater His impact will be upon your life. As you study His Word, He is speaking to you from His heart, teaching you how to live your life in such a way as to please Him in everything you think, say, and do.

It is important to our study that we understand that the Bible is God's Word. It is God's revelation of Himself to man. It is His letter to you. To get to know the God of the Word you must be in the Word of God, for it is there that we discover who He is. It is there that we find everything we need to live a godly life.

So, if you are going to be serious about removing the "I" from LIFE and living a life that glorifies God—a life that deeply and intimately understands God—you need to roll up your sleeves, grab your shovel and pickaxe, and begin digging into the Word of God. That is where you are going to find your answers.[39]

GIVE IT SOME THOUGHT
- ❏ Read Deuteronomy 10:12-13. What are the five things God desires from you?
  -
  -
  -
  -

- ❏ Why doesn't godliness automatically happen?

- ❏ Why do we so often try to achieve godliness in our own strength? What does that say about our hearts?

Endnotes

1. Romans 14:8
2. Ecclesiastes 2:11; see also 2:17, 21; 3:19
3. Isaiah 43:7; 1 Corinthians 10:31; Colossians 3:17; 1 Peter 4:11
4. Colossians 3:17
5. 1 Corinthians 10:31
6. Isaiah 55:2
7. Isaiah 49:4

8. Source unknown
9. Hebrews 11:6; Isaiah 40:31; 2 Corinthians 5:7
10. Ephesians 6:10-17
11. Philippians 2:3-11; James 4:6; 1 Peter 5:6
12. Matthew 5:8; 6:21; Psalm 119:9; Psalm 51:10; Proverbs 4:23
13. Romans 15:13; Deuteronomy 31:6; Isaiah 40:31; Psalm 39:7
14. Philippians 4:11-12; Hebrews 13:5; 1 Timothy 6:6-11; Proverbs 1:7; Psalm 111:10
15. 1 Timothy 6:11
16. Romans 8:25; 12:12; Galatians 6:9; Psalm 37:7-9
17. Titus 3:2; 2 Timothy 2:24-26; Proverbs 15:1; Ephesians 4:2
18. Proverbs 10:9; 11:3; 28:6
19. Psalm 24:8 (emphasis mine); compare with 1 Chronicles 29:11; Psalm 89:13; Ephesians 6:10; Jeremiah 50:34
20. Genesis 1
21. Psalm 147:4-5
22. Isaiah 45:7
23. Jeremiah 10:12
24. 1 Corinthians 6:14
25. Acts 2:24 (addition mine); compare with Acts 13:30, 37
26. See John 11:38-44; Mark 16:5-7; Acts 3:15; 1 Corinthians 15:3-8
27. 1 Chronicles 29:11-12 (emphasis mine)
28. Psalm 66:7
29. Psalm 46:10 (addition mine)
30. Hebrews 13:20-21
31. See Jeremiah 17:9-10; compare with Genesis 6:5; Psalm 53:1-3; Proverbs 28:26; Ecclesiastes 9:3; Matthew 15:19; Mark 7:21-22
32. John 3:30
33. 1 Corinthians 8:1
34. Psalm 51:16-17; compare with Hosea 6:6; Psalm 40:6, 8; Mark 12:33
35. Isaiah 55:11
36. 2 Timothy 3:7
37. James 1:22
38. John 5:39-40
39. 2 Timothy 3:16-17; Hebrews 4:12

> "Why do you call me, 'Lord, Lord,'
> and do not do what I say?"
> Luke 6:46

Three: Choosing your Choices

My kids grew up watching a children's program on television meant to be educational. One of the features of the show was a segment geared to help a child learn to identify what is out of place, what doesn't belong. It would show four items on the screen, then play a song saying that one of these things is not like the others. One of these things just doesn't belong. The child was then to choose which one it was.

Below is a list of four persons who are vying for the throne of your heart. Three of them are correct. One of these is not like the others, one just doesn't belong. Cross out the one that doesn't belong on the throne of *your* heart.
1. God the Father
2. God the Son
3. God the Holy Spirit
4. King Me

- ❑ Looking at that list above, why did you cross off the one you did? Why does that particular one not belong on the throne of your heart?

Sometimes—nah, let's admit it: most of the time—we aren't even aware of our King Me problem. We're so used to the King calling the shots that we don't notice what's happening. We're accustomed to making our own decisions, right or wrong, believing they are good choices. We're stuck in the rut of thinking we must always look out for number one because if we don't, who will?

You're being lied to, my friend. You've been duped into believing a colossal falsehood. You see, even though King Me is sitting on the throne of your heart, *you're* not calling the shots. It's not King Me who's actually in charge. You are just a puppet ruler. That's part of the deception of the enemy.

A puppet ruler is a person who has a title indicating possession of governmental power, but in reality, his actions are being dictated by an outside force. In other words, you think you're in charge. You believe you're making your own choices and decisions. You are convinced you're acting in your own best interest. However, you are being controlled by someone else. You're just his puppet.

The Devil doesn't care about you. Although he whispers in your ear that you're the head honcho and that what you say goes, he's just setting you up for failure. He has an agenda for you, and it's not one you're going to like. Why? He doesn't have your best interest at heart. In fact, Jesus said the Devil "comes only to steal and kill and destroy."[1] Does that sound like someone who truly cares about you and has your best as his goal? Satan wants nothing more than to use his crafty schemes to make you blind, stupid, and miserable.

The Devil is clever, coy, and manipulative—and he is a master liar.[2] He loves using lies and deceit to lead you off the straight path God wants you to walk, on to his twisted, dark, and sinister path that always leads to your destruction. He typically uses King Me to accomplish his dastardly deed.

The apostle Paul was well aware of the dangers Satan poses for all Christians. In fact, he was "afraid that just as Eve was deceived by the serpent's cunning, your minds may somehow be led astray from your sincere and pure devotion to Christ."[3] Paul knew that Satan's number one goal was to deceive you into believing that you're the King and you don't really need God.

Even though he is a master at deception, Satan doesn't have to "outwit us. For we are not unaware of his schemes."[4] Not only can we identify his various tricks, traps, and temptations, but we can skillfully avoid them as well.

The topic of this chapter is about choices—right choices. The choice is always yours. Whom are you going to serve: God or Satan? On the surface, for the Christian, this question seems to have a straightforward answer—God, of course! But think it through. Every day you're making a choice. Every moment of every day you're making a choice. When you are choosing not to follow God, when you are making a King Me decision, you are automatically choosing to follow the enemy.

❏ Write out Romans 6:16.

WAR—IT'S NOT A GAME

As I said in the introduction to this book, it's time to stage a coup. It's time to "submit yourselves, then, to God. Resist the devil," and God promises that when you do "he will flee from you."[5] It's time to place yourself under new leadership. It's time to choose to "fear the LORD and (choose to) serve him in sincerity and in faithfulness. Put away the god (King Me) (that you've been serving) and serve the LORD. And if it is evil in your eyes to serve the LORD, choose (right here and right now) whom you will serve...But as for me and my house, we will serve the LORD."[6]

> **Key Thought:** *Success in overthrowing the evil government of your heart requires the mindset of a warrior.*

We need to put the "war" back in warrior. Don't ever lose sight of the fact that we are daily engaged in intense spiritual warfare! You are to always and at all times "be strong in the Lord and in the strength of his might." Why? King Me won't win the battle—simply because King Me doesn't want to fight. The King likes where he is. The King has no intention of abdicating the throne.

If we are going to win this war, if we are going to dethrone and depose King Me and allow God to take His rightful place upon the throne of our hearts, we will need His strength, His wisdom, His guidance, and His leadership in our lives.

You see, "We do not wrestle against flesh and blood, but against the rulers, against the authorities, against the cosmic powers over this present darkness, against the spiritual forces of evil in the heavenly places. Therefore take up the whole armor of God, that you may be able to withstand in the evil day, and having done all, to stand firm."[7]

This is not a game, my friend. Our battle is against a very powerful, very clever, and crafty spiritual foe. That is why you are commanded, "Be self-controlled and alert. Your enemy the devil prowls around like a roaring lion looking for someone to devour. Resist him, standing firm in the faith."[8]

Satan is real. He loves to hide just under the surface of our everyday activities, clouded in mystery and confusion. As God told Cain in Genesis 4:7, "Sin is crouching at your door; it desires to have you, but you must master it."

How? How does a Christian master sin in his life? Take a few moments to ponder the following verses.
- "Be self-controlled and alert. Your enemy the devil prowls around like a roaring lion looking for someone to devour. Resist him, standing firm in the faith." (1 Peter 5:8-9a)

  Satan is public enemy #1 and he's out to destroy you. His plan? To lead you away from faith in God. He wants you to be full of self-confidence—*I've got this, I can handle this on my own, I don't need God*. When you allow yourself to sink in the mire of those thoughts, you lose control and are lulled into a false sense of security—exactly where he wants you to be.

Resist. Trust in God, not self. It is important in this battle that you are not letting King Me distract you. You must always be thinking clearly and correctly—King Me won't let you do that. You must, above all else, at any cost, protect your mind (see Proverbs 4:23). You must also be alert, constantly on the lookout for the tactics of the enemy. He wants to take you down, and just like a lion waiting in the tall grass, he *will* pounce without warning when you least expect it. So, trust not in King Me, but stand firm in your faith in God—and resist.

- "Finally, be strong in the Lord and in his mighty power. Put on the full armor of God so that you can take your stand against the devil's schemes." (Ephesians 6:10-11) Notice the promise that, through God's strength (not yours), you can take your stand against the enemy. We know his schemes. We know where he's hiding, and we know how he's going to attack. So, take your stand. In Christ you *can* do this![9]

- "Submit yourselves, then, to God. Resist the devil, and he will flee from you." (James 4:7) Did you catch the order of things here? You must first choose to submit to God. Choose to allow him to sit on the throne of your heart. You are not king—He is. You will never know victory until you first choose surrender.

Once you have submitted, once you have chosen to allow God full reign in your heart, then and only then can you effectively resist the devil, standing in complete opposition to him—and he will flee from you! Satan won't respond to a puppet king, but he will flee from the King of all kings!

- "But the Lord is faithful, and he will strengthen and protect you from the evil one." (2 Thessalonians 3:3)

  It's vital that you not lose sight of the fact that it is the Lord who gives you the strength, the ability, and the confidence to stand firm against the enemy of your soul. Not King Me, but God.

- "You, dear children, are from God and have overcome them, because the one who is in you is greater than the one who is in the world." (1 John 4:4)

- "No, in all these things we are more than conquerors through him who loved us. For I am convinced that neither death nor life, neither angels nor demons, neither the present nor the future, nor any powers, neither height nor depth, nor anything else in all creation, will be able to separate us from the love of god that is in Christ Jesus our Lord." (Romans 8:37-39)

Let me repeat this crucial point: King Me cannot win this fight. "No king is saved by the size of his army; no warrior escapes by his great strength. A horse is a vain hope for deliverance; despite all its great strength it cannot save."[10]

DETHRONING AND DEPOSING THE KING
❑ Write out Ephesians 6:13.

❑ According to Ephesians 6:13, what does God promise will come when I put on His armor?

❑ When that "evil day" comes, what two things are you supposed to do?

❑ Why do we have to fight? Why can't the Christian life be easy?

In a monarchy, to dethrone a king (removing him from the place of power and authority) and to depose him (making sure he doesn't retake the throne) takes nothing short of a revolution. In the timeline of every revolution in history, there has always been a critical moment when there is a direct confrontation between the old regime and the new. It's inevitable. There is a direct challenge of the power and authority of the old leadership. Typically, the reigning monarch doesn't go down without a fight—many times violent and bloody warfare follows.

Dethroning King Me isn't just a one-and-done thing. King Me won't go away that easily. You can't just wake up one morning and say, "Okay, Your Highness, strike three, you're outta here!" It doesn't work that way. It would be nice—great, even—but unh-unh, not gonna happen.

As long as you take breath, King Me is going to hound you. The King likes the throne. The King craves the attention. The King wants to remain king and will fight you tooth and nail to retain his title as king of your heart. So, dethroning and deposing King Me is going to be messy, exhausting, and frustrating. However, it can be done, and it's worth the fight.

LIVE DAILY BY GOD'S WORD
Notice I didn't say just read your Bible. Reading God's Word is good—it's very good; but just reading your Bible isn't going to set

up a defense around the throne strong enough to keep King Me from trying to take it back. No, you can't just read it; you must live it.

> **Key Thought:** *God's Word is a window to your soul. It will show you what's in your heart. You must then act.*

❑ Write out Hebrews 4:12.

❑ According to Hebrews 4:12, what are the things God's Word is and does?

Think about this for a moment. God's Word is "living" and it is "active." Peter calls it "living and enduring,"[11] and Paul told the church at Thessalonica that it is always "at work in you who believe."[12] Every time you read it, every time you hear it, every time you meditate on it, it is actively at work in your heart. It's always accomplishing something.[13]

We also see in our text that it always penetrates to the heart of the matter. "Is not my word like fire, declares the Lord, and like a hammer that breaks the rock in pieces?"[14] Too often we make choices that aren't governed by Scripture because we're easily caught up in all the frill and fluff that this world has to offer. God's Word burns past all that stuff, it breaks it into smithereens, and it speaks directly to your mind.

Living by the Word of God means you are reading it, you're studying it, you're meditating (thinking) on it, *and* you are obeying it—all of it. "You shall therefore love the Lord your God and keep his charge, his statutes, his rules, and his commandments always!"[15]

❑ Do you love God?

- ❏ In what ways is your life currently supporting your answer?

- ❏ In what ways is your life not supporting your answer?

How do we actively demonstrate our love for God? Jesus answers with this: "If you love me, you will keep my commandments."[16] In other words, obedience. King Me must choose to abdicate the throne in deference to the real King. "Whoever has my commands and obeys them, he is the one who loves me."[17] "If anyone loves me, he will obey my teaching."[18]

> **Key Thought:** *To keep King Me off the throne of your heart, open your Bible daily. Study it. Dig deep. Meditate on it—think not only about what it's saying, but what God wants you to do about it. Memorize it. Obey it.*

WALK DAILY BY THE SPIRIT
- ❏ Write out Galatians 5:16.

- ❏ What is the choice God wants you to make?

- ❏ What are the promised consequences of making that specific choice?

I want you to notice in this verse that Paul is stating that as a Christian you have two primary drives—the Holy Spirit and the flesh (see Romans 7:15-25). The Spirit produces within you one kind of desire—namely, the desire to please God. "Those who live according to the Spirit set their minds on the things of the Spirit."[19]

When we walk by the Spirit we aren't controlled by the sinful desires of the flesh. We are choosing instead to yield to the desire the Spirit has created within us to please God. That's what Paul is referring to in Romans 7 when he says, "I have the desire to do what is right" (v.18), and "I delight in the law of God, in my inner being" (v.22).

❏ Write out Romans 8:8.

The flesh, on the other hand, produces a different kind of desire. That desire is completely contrary to the one the Spirit creates—namely, the desire to please self. The Spirit is all about God. The flesh doesn't care about God, only about its own sinful pleasures.

Again, I refer back to Romans 7. Paul clearly states that "nothing good dwells in me, that is, in my flesh" (v.18). Because the flesh is against God, "I have the desire to do what is right, but not the ability to carry it out" (v.18). As we just saw in Romans 8:8, when I am in the flesh, living for King Me, I cannot please God.

This is the ongoing battle that Paul talks about in Romans 7:15-25. In Galatians 5:17 he describes it this way: "For the desires of the flesh are against the Spirit, and the desires of the Spirit are against the flesh, for these are opposed to each other, to keep you from doing the things you want to do."

This is why we are instructed to "walk by the Spirit." In other words, daily choose to conduct your life according to the leading of the Spirit, not the passions (or "works") of the flesh. The "works of the flesh" are what you do when you "gratify the desires of the flesh" (see Galatians 5:19-21).

When I choose to give in to the sinful desires that constantly plague me, I allow King Me to climb back up on the throne. I am choosing to ignore the desires of the Holy Spirit in favor of the desires of my flesh.

Okay, great—I need to walk by the Spirit, but how?
Step 1: I Must Surrender
- ❏ In battle, when an opposing force surrenders, what are they doing? What are they saying?

In the battle for the throne of your heart, you must first surrender to God. You must acknowledge deep in the core of your being that you are totally and completely helpless to do good (to honor and glorify God) on your own—you need God's help.

> **Key Thought**: *There can be no victory where there is no surrender.*

- ❏ Write out John 15:5.

- ❏ According to the last part of this verse, what is King Me capable of doing? Why?

Now, of course King Me is capable of doing something without Christ—I can sin. But that's all I can do. Even when King Me is doing something "good," what's the ultimate goal? Who are you really doing it for? The answer: King Me. That is idolatry. That is worshiping someone other than God, and that is sin.

So, the first step in walking by the Spirit is to surrender. Acknowledge and admit that you can't do it—you've tried before and failed. It's denying yourself, taking up your cross daily, and following Christ.[20] It's acknowledging that God is our Father. We are nothing but clay in the hands of the potter—we are totally the work of His hand.[21]

An Example of Surrender
❏ Write out Psalm 25:1.

Take a moment here and think about what David is saying. "To you, O Lord, I lift up my soul." That's such a simple phrase that we tend to skip over it, looking for something else that has more depth, more "meat" to it. But I want us to stop here for a moment and consider what we just read.

What is David doing in verse one? If you answered something like "lifting up his soul," you would be correct. But what do you think that means? Furthermore, why is he doing that?

First, I want you to notice that David is making a choice. He is choosing to lift up his soul. He is choosing to surrender his life to the Lord. This wasn't something being forced upon him. He was doing this of his own volition. He was willingly choosing to surrender his life to God.

I have a question for you: Are you making that same choice? Notice I didn't ask "have you made" or "will you make," as if it's a one-and-done thing. This is a daily, moment-by-moment decision that you must continuously make. Are you daily making that choice?

"To you, O Lord, I lift up my soul." We must repeatedly choose to lift up our souls to the Almighty, most Sovereign Creator and God of the Universe. You are who you are (a child of God) because God is who He is (the Savior of your soul). You owe God everything.

Second, notice what David is choosing. He is lifting up his soul. In other words, he is choosing to sacrifice King Me to the King of Kings. That's what I need to do—daily. I need to kneel before God's altar, head bowed, eyes closed, hands lifted high, with my beating heart—pulsating with life—in the palms of my hands as I choose to surrender it willingly and completely to my Heavenly Father.

David is choosing to surrender his soul, totally, completely, unreservedly to God. In essence he is saying, "God, *you* are King. Not me, but YOU! You are Lord over every aspect of my life. You are Lord over my thoughts. You are Lord over my words. You are Lord over my choices. You are Lord over my actions."

Don't miss the significance of David's confession. David is the #1 dude in all of Israel. He's the alpha dog, the head honcho, the king! He is the lord (master) of the children of Israel. What he says goes. What he wants happens. All of Israel looks to him for guidance, direction, and protection.

By calling God his "Lord" (Jehovah), David is confessing that there is One even greater than him, One to whom he is ultimately answerable. King Me does not belong on the throne—God does. Can you say that? Is God your Lord, not just in word, but in your attitude and behavior as well? Is He the ruler and master of every aspect of your life, every moment of your life? Does he have ultimate reign over your soul?

By the way, David uses the term "lift up" in the imperfect tense. That means that the action being described is still happening, because it is not yet complete; it's imperfect. So, David is saying that the lifting up of his soul—the choice to totally and completely surrender every part of his life to God—is an ongoing, daily thing.

❏ Why must this be done daily? Why can't it be a one-and-done kind of thing?

Third, notice specifically what it is that David is lifting up to God: his soul. The word "soul" here refers to one's appetites, desires, emotions, and passions—the core of all you are. David is declaring to God his intent to fully yield everything to God.
- God, today I choose to surrender all of my appetites for _____ completely to you!
- God, today I choose to surrender all of my desires for _____ completely to you!
- God, today I choose to surrender all of my emotions completely to you!
- God, today I choose to surrender all of my passions completely to you!

Don't lose sight of the fact that *King* David is writing this declaration of surrender. This is important. You see, a king doesn't retreat. A king doesn't yield. A king doesn't surrender. After all, he's the king. Everyone else yields to him, retreats before him, surrenders to him. That makes this simple declaration—"To you, O Lord, I lift up my soul"—powerful beyond imagination.

What about you? When King Me is sitting on the throne of your heart you don't want to retreat. You don't want to yield. You don't want to surrender. After all, you're the king. Everyone else should yield to you, retreat before you, surrender to you.

Just as King David did, King Me needs to cry out, "To you, O Lord, I lift up my soul." We need to say, "God, I surrender. I come before your altar and humbly kneel before the almighty, most holy God of the Universe. I choose to completely surrender all of my appetites, desires, emotions, and passions over to you. All that makes me who and what I am, I willingly and fully hand over to you."

Now, if we're being totally honest, that's a frightening proposition. Surrendering every part of your life over to God can be a scary thing, right?
- ❏ Why are we afraid of lifting up our souls to God?

This is why the next step is so crucial.

Step 2: I Must Trust
- ❏ Write out Psalm 25:2.

Once again, think carefully about what David is saying here—"Oh my God, in you I trust!" David had just made a significant sacrifice. He had knelt before the King of kings and surrendered his entire being, his entire heart, his entire life over to God.

Let's pause for a moment here to understand how God views the promises you make to Him.
- "When a man makes a vow to the Lord or takes an oath to obligate himself by a pledge, he must not break his word but must do everything he said." (Numbers 30:2)
- "If you make a vow to the Lord your God, do not be slow to pay it, for the Lord your God will certainly demand it of you and you will be guilty of sin." (Deuteronomy 23:21)
- "Whatever your lips utter you must be sure to do, because you made your vow freely to the Lord your God with your own mouth." (Deuteronomy 23:23)
- "You will pray to him, and he will hear you, and you will fulfill your vows." (Job 22:27)
- "When you make a vow to God, do not delay in fulfilling it. He has no pleasure in fools; fulfill your vow. It is better not to vow than to make a vow and not fulfill it. Do not let your mouth lead you into sin. And do not protest...'My vow was

a mistake.' Why should God be angry at what you say and destroy the work of your hands?" (Ecclesiastes 5:4-6)

David understood the ramifications of his personal commitment to God. "O Lord, I lift up, I surrender, I fully yield all control of my soul, my life to you." David didn't make that vow lightly. God didn't take that vow lightly.

So, David then cries out to God, "In you I trust!" In essence he was saying, "God, I meant what I just said; now I need your help to accomplish it!"

Sometimes believing in God is the easy part. Believing in his plan for our lives is often much, much harder. Why? It requires trust in Him. Not just in His existence, but *in Him*.
❏ Why do so many Christians struggle with trusting in God?

Imagine two college students going out on their first date. As they sit across from each other enjoying their pizza, she looks deeply into his eyes, smiles, and says, "I want full access to your bank account, the keys to your car, and all your passwords." How do you think he would react? Any sane guy is going to say, "No way, princess! Not in your wildest dreams is that going to happen!" Why? Because he doesn't trust her.

Now let me ask you this: Why doesn't he trust her? Simply put, he doesn't trust her because he doesn't yet know her. How does he get to know her? He must intentionally invest time daily to be around her, listen to her, learn about her, study her, talk with her, and bask in her company. As he develops an understanding of her, as he begins to truly know her heart and her character, he then begins to trust her.

It's the same way with God. God is looking deeply into your eyes, and with a warm loving smile says, "I want full access to your heart

—every nook and cranny, every desire, every passion, every thought and every decision. I want it all." Many times we struggle with that. Why? Because we don't trust Him. And why don't we trust Him? Because we don't really know Him.

> "Those who know your name put their trust in you,
> for you, O Lord, have not forsaken those who seek you." (Psalm 9:10)

How well do you know God? To answer that question, we must first dig into these questions:
- How much time to you invest each day with God?
- How often do you read your Bible and listen to Him talking to you?
- When you are reading your Bible, how deep do you go?
- What is your goal in reading Scripture? (Is it just to do your Christian duty, or to really get to know your Heavenly Father?)
- How often do you truly pray, talking with God? I'm not referring to a "now I lay me down to sleep" or "rub-a-dub-dub, thanks for the grub" kind of "prayer." I'm referring to a down-on-your-knees, humbly (yet boldly[22]) coming into the presence of the thrice-holy God to just talk to Him—not to ask for anything, just to talk.

When King Me is sitting on the throne, your tendency is to "boast in your wisdom" and "boast in your might" and "boast in your riches." "But let him who boasts boast in this, that he understands and knows me, that I am the Lord who practices steadfast love, justice, and righteousness in the earth. For in these things I delight, declares the Lord."[23]

> **Key Thought:** *How well do you know God? The answer is revealed in how much you trust Him!*

You're probably familiar with the words of Proverbs 3:5-6 that command us, "Trust in the Lord with all your heart, and do not lean on your own understanding. In all your ways acknowledge him, and he will make straight your paths." That's not just a nice suggestion, it's a command—trust in the Lord with ALL your heart. For that to happen you must "grow in the grace and knowledge of our Lord and Savior Jesus Christ."[24]

The main question we've been examining in this chapter is this: How do I not only dethrone King Me, but keep myself off the throne for good? We've seen that we must live daily by God's Word, and we must walk daily by God's Spirit. To walk by the Spirit I must first surrender, then I must trust.

Step 3: I Must Obey
Something has drastically shifted in Christianity. Collectively, as a body of believers, we have lost a respect for the law—God's law. I'm not saying that we are blatantly throwing it out the window with a "do whatever floats your boat" attitude. I'm not saying that we are acting like we don't care what God thinks anymore (although I do believe that is happening in some Christian circles). I am referring to a smorgasbord mentality when it comes to our Bible.

We treat God's Word like a buffet table, reading Scripture, then picking and choosing which laws and standards we like. We then choose to obey and follow them, leaving the rest to the "irrelevance of Old Testament times," believing that God no longer means this or demands that.

In Psalm 19:7 David makes a powerful statement about God's Word. "The law of the Lord is perfect!" All of God's law is perfect. Is that how you view the Bible? Can you say "the law of (God's) mouth is better to me than thousands of gold and silver pieces"?[25] Another way to put that verse is like this: God's Word is better to me than (name something that King Me loves and doesn't want to give up).
Can you honestly cry out, "Oh how I love your law! It is my meditation all the day"?[26] If you want genuine and lasting victory over the reign of King Me in your heart, dig into your Bible. "Read in it all the days of (your) life…learn to fear the Lord (your) God by (obeying) all the words of (God's) law and these statutes, and (do) them."[27]

My friend, don't let "this Book of the Law...depart from your mouth, but...meditate on it day and night, so that you may be careful to *do* according to all that is written in it. For then you will make your way prosperous"[28]—and then you will successfully dethrone and depose King Me!

❏ What role does obedience play in trusting God—and why?

❏ Read James 2:14-26. According to this passage, how do you know a person trusts God? (circle one)

By what they say.   By what they do.

Are you *doing* what God wants you to do? God has a code of conduct for His children, a certain behavior He expects from each of us. God's code of conduct gives us the tools we need to unseat King Me and maintain a close relationship with Him. They are God's boundaries that give us an amazing freedom in serving Him—when we choose to obey them.

Please don't look at Scripture as a set of rules handed to you by a tyrant of a God who is distant, detached, and doesn't care about you. Don't view God as someone who is sitting up in Heaven just waiting for you to screw up, so He can zap you. Your Bible isn't a disciplinary manual filled with dos and don'ts.

In 2 Chronicles we see that King Uzziah "did what was right in the eyes of the Lord...as long as he sought the Lord, God gave him success."[29] Your battle is not with God. Your fight is not with the King of kings and Lord of lords. The battle is with your flesh—King Me wanting to dominate your life. When you dethrone and depose the king for the purpose of bringing honor and glory to God, He promises to give you "rest on every side."[30]

When I pursue anything but God in my life, I make myself, my goals, my desires, and my wants—even my fears—a "god" in my life. I give King Me exactly what he wants. What I worship is what I will serve. God is abundantly clear that serving anything or anyone other than Him is unacceptable.[31]

FOR KING AND GLORY

Never forget and never lose sight of the fact that it's not about King Me! It's not about *you* having victory or *you* winning the war. Whatever you do, whenever you do it, choose always and only to do all for God's glory.

We will never find real freedom from that dastardly, domineering, and deceitful dictator (known as King Me) until our primary reason for wanting it is so that we can glorify God. As long as it is about us, we will snatch the glory for our self.

It is said of King Hezekiah, "In everything that he undertook…he sought his God and worked wholeheartedly. And so he prospered."[32] King Hezekiah dethroned King Me and allowed God to reign in his heart. And so he prospered.

Listen closely: In everything you do, in every aspect of this life, you must seek God's strength, God's wisdom, and God's glory. Only then will you prosper.

Endnotes

1. John 10:10
2. John 8:44
3. 2 Corinthians 10:3
4. 2 Corinthians 2:11
5. James 4:7
6. Joshua 24:14-15 (additions mine)
7. Ephesians 6:10-13
8. 1 Peter 5:8-9a
9. Philippians 4:13
10. Psalm 33:16-17 (NIV '84); compare with Psalm 44:2-3, 6-8

11. 1 Peter 1:23 (NIV '84)
12. 1 Thessalonians 2:13
13. Isaiah 55:11
14. Jeremiah 23:29
15. Deuteronomy 11:1
16. John 14:15
17. John 14:21 (NIV '84)
18. John 14:23 (NIV '84)
19. Romans 8:5
20. Matthew 16:24-25
21. Isaiah 64:8
22. Hebrews 4:16
23. Jeremiah 9:23-24
24. 2 Peter 3:18
25. Psalm 119:72 (addition mine)
26. Psalm 119:97
27. Deuteronomy 17:19 (additions mine)
28. Joshua 1:8 (emphasis mine)
29. 2 Chronicles 26:4-5
30. 2 Chronicles 14:7
31. Exodus 20:3; compare with Deuteronomy 5:7; 6:5, 14; Joshua 24:23
32. 2 Chronicles 31:21 (NIV '84)

"And whatever you do, in word or deed, do everything in the name of the Lord Jesus, giving thanks to God the Father through him."
Colossians 3:17

Four: A Glorious Game-Changer

God, and God alone, is worthy "to receive glory and honor and power."[1] "Everything comes from him and exists by his power and is intended for his glory."[2]

❏ Do you truly believe the statement above?

❏ Does your attitude and daily behavior support your answer?

❏ If you truly believe that only God is worthy to receive your glory, honor, and praise, then your life will be a daily reflection of that. Let me ask you this: Why is God alone worthy of *all* glory and honor?

Now, I have an important question for you. Do you *want* to live a life that draws people to God? I'm not asking if you think it's a good

Removing the "I" from Life

idea. I'm not inquiring into your personal opinion on the matter. I'm asking flat out: Do you want to glorify God in your life?

❏ Write out 1 Corinthians 10:31.

Take a moment and meditate on the verse you just wrote. No matter what you do, when you do it, or where it's being done, always do it for God's glory. Just think about that. God is not expecting us to live a life that occasionally, or even mostly, glorifies Him. Every aspect of your life, every moment of every day, is to be lived in a way that He (and He alone) receives recognition, praise, and honor.

Now that's a tall order. I mean, living a life that in every way and at all times glorifies God is certainly a noble and holy endeavor. But is it really possible? Can you actually function in a way that *every* thought, *every* word, and *every* action is in *every* way reflecting to the world around you the absolute greatness, majesty, wonder, and supremacy of the Almighty God of the Universe? My answer to you is, yes—yes you can! (See Philippians 4:13.)

I SEE YOU!
Have you ever had that eerie feeling that someone's watching you? You whip your head around to see who it is, only to discover that there isn't anyone there, or that the people around you aren't even looking your way. Creepy.

The fact is, people are watching and observing your life every day. In my younger years I did a fair amount of stage acting. One thing my director drilled into our minds was the fact that at all times on that stage—whether you have a speaking line or not—people *are* watching you. This is a great lesson for life as well. No matter what you may (or may not) be doing, people *are* watching you.

- Titus 2:7-8 instructs us to "show yourself in all respects to be a model of good works, and…show integrity, dignity, and sound speech that cannot be condemned." Why? Because people are watching you.

- Jesus said in Matthew 5:14-16 that "you are the light of the world. A city set on a hill cannot be hidden. Nor do people light a lamp and put it under a basket, but on a stand, and it gives light to all in the house. In the same way, let your light shine before others, so that they may see your good works and give glory to your Father who is in heaven." People are watching you.
- Peter challenges us to "keep your conduct ... honorable, so that ... they may see your good deeds and glorify God" (1 Peter 2:12). Yes, people are watching you.
- And in 1 Timothy 4:12, Paul said we are to "set an example in speech, in conduct, in love, in faith, in purity." Hopefully by now you understand that people are watching you.
- ❏ Write out 1 Peter 3:15.

Too often we emphasize the wrong thing in our Christian walk. Too often we focus on being prepared to share the Gospel, being ready to speak out for our faith. Don't misunderstand— yes, we must be able to stand up for what we believe. However, if I am not living out what I believe, how will anyone ever know to ask me to share what I believe and why I believe it?

It's only when you daily choose to surrender yourself completely to God that your life will be a reflection of the God you serve. So, think carefully about what God is telling us here. People are watching you. People are observing your life. As they look at how you live, how you react and respond to life, what are they seeing? What kind of God are you portraying to them?

❏ As people watch me, are they getting a right view of God?

- ❏ Am I making a lasting impression upon them for the Kingdom of Heaven?

- ❏ In what ways does a person's concept of God impact their life?

- ❏ How does *your* concept of God impact:
  - Your relationship with your spouse (or your choice of one, if single)?

  - Your relationship with your children (or your nephews and nieces, etc.)?

  - Your family and friends?

  - Your co-workers?

  - Your church family?

As people watch your life, *they are seeing* how you view God. How you relate to, and interact with, God on a daily basis will be reflected in every word you speak and everything you do.
- What are your family, friends, co-workers, and neighbors understanding about God as they listen to your words and observe your actions?
- Are you a mirror reflecting Him, or a wall hiding Him?
- Do you let your light shine for all to see, or are you hiding it somewhere deep within?
- Do people see the image of King Me that you have worked so hard to refine and polish, or do they see the image of Christ being lived out?
- Do you stand up for Him, even when you may stand alone?

> **Key Thought:** *Only when we set apart Christ as Lord in our hearts will He show up as Lord in our lives.*

SO, IN CONCLUSION
"Now all has been heard; here is the conclusion of the matter: Fear God and keep his commandments, for this is the whole duty of man. For God will bring every deed into judgment, including every hidden thing, whether it is good or evil."[3]

> **Key Thought:** *Meaning and purpose to life is found only when we focus our entire being around glorifying God.*

I challenge you to re-read that key thought. Peter reminds us that in all things—in *all* things—God is to be glorified.[4] Never forget that God formed you, He made you, He created you for the purpose of bringing Him glory.[5]

Let's dig a little deeper into that for a moment. God specifically designed you to glorify Him in everything you think, say, and do. It has been programmed within your very DNA. As a result, true purpose and meaning to life is found only when you are doing that which God created you to do.[6]
- Are you functioning according to The Manufacturer's specs?
- Are you consistently living a life that glorifies Him?[7]

- Are you daily walking in complete surrender[8] and total obedience to your Heavenly Father at all times?[9]

Let me remind you of what 1 Corinthians 10:31 says: "So whether you eat or drink or whatever you do, do it all for the glory of God." Now zero in on the word "all" for a moment. Do you remember our definition of that word in Chapter Three? "All" means all and that's all "all" means!

- ❏ So according to 1 Corinthians 10:31, how much of your life is to glorify God?

Never forget the fact that God is all about His glory—not ours. God says, "For my own sake, for my own sake I do this. How can I let myself be defamed? I will not yield my glory to another."[10] When we seek our own praise and glory, we are dethroning God and setting up King Me in His place. God will not tolerate that. "I am the Lord; that is my name! I will not give my glory to another or my praise to idols."[11]

- ❏ Write the words of Colossians 3:17.

I challenge you to look carefully at the way Colossians 3:17 is written. There is no option here. Whatever you do, *do it* in Jesus' name. Paul isn't saying here, "Hey, it sure would be nice if you would try your best to glorify God more often than not in your life." Unh-unh. He is expressing God's expectation of His children. *Everything* you say and *everything* you do in life is to be said and done in Jesus' name! Not just some of the things you say and most of the things you do … everything. Ouch!

- ❏ How are you doing with that?

There are some important truths in Colossians 3:17 I do not want you to miss. For example, notice that Paul starts this verse by using the word "whatever." Let me take a moment and remind you that every word of God is inspired.[12] In fact, Jesus Himself said that every letter used in Scripture to spell out the words comes directly from God.[13] That means that even that simple word "whatever" in Colossians 3:17 is inspired and therefore important; worthy of our attention.

As Paul writes the words "whatever you do," he is referring to exactly what you would understand that phrase to mean. He's pointing to the sum total of each and every thing that you say or do, each and every time you speak it or do it. Nothing—not even a single part of a thing—is to be left out of this equation.

The words "whatever you do, whether in word or deed," are telling us that each and every individual word we say, as well as each and every particular activity we do—all of it, every part of it—must always be said and done to the glory of God. If they are not glorifying Him, we are sinning.

❏ How often do you closely examine your words and actions—before ever speaking them or doing them—to make sure that each and every one glorifies God?

Remember, God is not a liar.[14] That means you can do this—through Christ you can ensure that every word and every action, every moment of every day, glorifies God!

WORD, SCHMERD — WHAT'S THE BIG DEAL?
Look again at our verse in Colossians 3:17, and let's break it down even further.

"Whatever (we) do, whether in word or deed, (we are to) do it all in the name of the Lord Jesus, giving thanks to God the Father through Him."

Keeping in mind what we just discussed regarding the word "whatever," notice that Paul uses that word to describe our daily speech. Whatever you do in word—whatever you may say—say it all in the name of the Lord Jesus.

Each and every word that comes out of your mouth, *whatever* the words may be and *whatever* the reason for saying them—no matter to whom you're speaking them or what you're trying to say—is to be spoken in a way that glorifies God. Simply put, your "speech (should) *always* be gracious, seasoned with salt, so that you may know how you ought to answer each person."[15]

Take a quick stroll through the book of Proverbs. On this little walk, I want you to notice along the way what God says about the words that come out of your mouth.
- "When words are many, sin is not absent, but he who holds his tongue is wise."[16]
- "Reckless words pierce like a sword, but the tongue of the wise brings healing."[17]
- "He who guards his lips guards his life, but he who speaks rashly will come to ruin."[18]
- "The tongue of the wise commends knowledge, but the mouth of the fool gushes folly."[19]
- "The tongue that brings healing is a tree of life, but a deceitful tongue crushes the spirit."[20]
- "A wise man's heart guides his mouth, and his lips promote instruction. Pleasant words are a honeycomb, sweet to the soul."[21]
- "A man of knowledge uses words with restraint."[22]
- "Even a fool is thought wise if he keeps silent, and discerning if he holds his tongue."[23]
- "He who guards his mouth and his tongue keeps himself from calamity."[24]
- "A word aptly spoken is like apples of gold in settings of silver."[25]

After this very brief glance through just one book of the Bible, would you agree that God wants us to be careful with our words?[26]

Always consider what you say, my friend, because God does.[27] Every time you open your mouth to speak, before a single word comes out, ask God to "set a guard over (your) mouth" and "keep watch over the door of (your) lips."[28] Cry out to Him, "Father, please 'let the words of my mouth and the meditation of my heart be acceptable in your sight, O LORD, my Rock and my Redeemer'."[29] You see, every one of us "will have to give account on the Day of Judgment for every careless word (we) have spoken."[30]

Consider with me for a moment what Christ says in Luke 6:45. "A good man brings good things out of the good stored up in his heart, and an evil man brings evil things out of the evil stored up in his heart. For *the mouth speaks what the heart is full of*" (emphasis mine).

> **Key Thought:** *Good speech (words that will glorify God) comes from a good heart—from a heart that is always focused on glorifying God.*

❑ Think about the language you use each day. Think about the words you say. What are your words revealing about your heart?

However, if your heart is focused on self instead of God—if your inner goal is to make King Me happy—your words (and the motivation of your heart for saying those words) will be all about self, not God.

LET THE INTERROGATION BEGIN
To glorify God in your everyday speech, you must continuously evaluate the real reason why you're using *that* particular word to construct *that* particular sentence to make *that* particular point; and then you need to make the necessary adjustments to what you're going to say.
- Why are you saying what you are to your spouse?
- What is the real reason for talking to your children that way?

- What is the ultimate goal in wording things the way you do to your boss or co-worker?
- Why did you tell your friends that particular story?

Your words expose what is in your heart.[31]

Our tendency at this point is to think that there's no way we can do that. *"EVERY word EVERY moment of EVERY day? C'mon Steve, you're asking the impossible. I speak thousands of words daily! It just can't be done."* I agree with you—without God's help, it is impossible.

Our problem lies in the fact that we are accustomed to talking without putting much thought into what we're saying. Or, when we do think through what we're going to say, glorifying God with our words isn't top on our priority list.

The concept of thinking through everything you say before you speak, so that each of your words bring honor to God, feels completely foreign and totally impossible. The exciting thing is that God has created us as creatures of habit. Repetitive action eventually forms habitual action. Yes, it's work now, but it won't always be.

With God's help, you can "keep (your) tongue from evil and (your) lips from deceitful speech."[32] It truly is possible to consistently restrain your tongue from saying things that will not glorify God. But how? How do you keep from saying things that glorify self instead of God? The answer begins in your mind.

SPEAK YOUR MIND AND MIND YOUR SPEECH
In Matthew 12, Jesus is addressing the sinful condition of the heart of the Pharisees. In verse 34 He states, "Out of the overflow of the heart the mouth speaks." Your words—*every* word—and the motivation behind each word, reveal what is in your heart.

Let's take this a bit deeper. You see, the word that Jesus uses for "heart" isn't referring to that muscle that goes thumpety-thump in your chest. No, He is speaking about the core of who you are. It is "command central," if you will. It is the place where your thoughts, passions, desires, affections, and decision-making all occur: your mind.

Your words are a direct result of what is going on in your thoughts. What you think will come out in what you say.

> **Key Thought:** *If your thoughts are centered on King Me, your words will be focused on King Me.*

The prophet Isaiah said that the man whose mind is busy with evil will speak folly (Isaiah 32:6). Conversely, if your thoughts are focused on God, your words will draw attention to Him.

A great example of this is King David. I encourage you to read through the Psalms with this concept in mind. David kept his mind focused on God. As a result he was able to say, "My mouth is filled with your praise, declaring your splendor all day long."[33] "My tongue shall tell of your righteousness and of your praise all the day long."[34]

Ask yourself this question—and answer honestly:
- ❏ Does each and every word I speak, and the motivation behind them, bring glory to God?

- ❏ When I am speaking to my spouse, to my children, to my employer or employees, to my co-workers, to my family members, to my friends and neighbors, even to those annoying telemarketers, am I considering carefully everything I am saying to be sure each and every word is glorifying God?

❏ Since your words reveal what is in your thoughts, the real question is: Do your thoughts truly glorify God?

WALKING IN THE DO DO DO

Not only should every word we speak glorify God, but everything we *do* must glorify Him as well. In Colossians 3:17 Paul goes on to say, "Whatever you do in word *or deed*," do it all with the goal of glorifying God.

What exactly is a "deed" and how do I make it glorify God? Usually we think of a deed as a specific activity or task that we accomplish. For example, we may volunteer to help out in the nursery at church, join a group of people on a short-term mission trip, or rake an elderly neighbor's leaves. It certainly can, and does, include those things, but that simple word, "deed," in Colossians 3:17 refers to so much more. A "deed" can incorporate something as simple as crossing your arms to make a point, rolling your eyes, sighing loudly, or offering a friendly pat on the back for encouragement. Did you ever consider the fact that even your body language should glorify God?

When you stop to think about it, this is a very powerful word! It refers to each and every individual thing we do—including our body language—no matter how insignificant we may think it is. Even the raising of an eyebrow, the shrug of our shoulders, the glaring of our eyes, the shaking of our head, or a simple smile of encouragement is considered by God to be a deed that should be done in the name of Jesus Christ.

It is also important for us to realize that these deeds are not referring only to the ones seen by men. It refers to each and every deed—whether in public *or in private*. Scripture tells us that "God will bring *every deed* into judgment, with every secret thing, whether good or evil."[35] So even the "hidden" things you say and do when

you're all by yourself are still to be said and done to the glory of God.
- What are you watching? Does it glorify God?
- What are you listening to? Does it glorify God?
- What are you reading? Does it glorify God?
- What activities are you participating in? Do they glorify God?

Jesus said, "Nothing (is) concealed that will not be disclosed, or hidden that will not be made known. What you have said in the dark will be heard in the daylight, and what you have whispered in the ear in the inner rooms will be proclaimed from the roofs."[36] You see, God's "eyes are on all (our) ways; they are not hidden from (Him), nor is (our) iniquity concealed from (His) eyes."[37]

Our secret sins will be exposed in the light of His presence.[38] This is because "nothing in all creation is hidden from God's sight. Everything is uncovered and laid bare before the eyes of him to whom we must give account."[39]

1 Samuel 2:3 tells us that "the LORD is a God who knows, and by Him deeds are weighed." In 1 Chronicles 28:9 we read that "the LORD searches every heart and understands every motive behind the thoughts" (NIV '84). Consider both of those verses carefully. God knows each and every one of your deeds, public and private. While this is true, these verses reveal something more, something much deeper. God not only knows your deeds but the motivation of your heart behind each deed. He not only knows what you did, He also knows why you did it.

Paul warns us that God "will bring to light what is hidden in darkness and will expose the *motives* of men's hearts."[40] We do what we do because in our hearts we want what we want. What is your heart wanting? Is it wanting to glorify God, or to please self?

Passing the Exam

In Jeremiah 17:10 God says, "I the LORD search the heart and test the mind, to give every man according to his ways, according to the fruit of his deeds." Whoa ... wait a minute, did you catch that?

> **Key Thought:** *On the scales of God's justice your deeds are seriously considered, but God places more weight on your heart's motivation, on the thoughts you were thinking as you did each deed. He looks not just at the what, but the why.*

Look again at Jeremiah 17:10 above. God searches your heart and *examines your mind*. Yes, your deed is important to God, but even more so is the reason behind it—that which was going on in your thoughts as you did it. He is not going to reward your deed, no matter how great it might be, if the thoughts and motivation behind it was wrong. What you think will become what you do.

> **Key Thought:** *In order for your deeds and actions to glorify God, your thoughts must glorify Him.*

Just as with your words, your deeds reveal what is in your heart. Proverbs 23:7 says that "as (a man) thinketh in his heart, so is he" (KJV). What you think will eventually become what you do. That means your words and your actions are clear indications of who is sitting on the throne of your heart. All anyone has to do is look at the things you do, and listen to the words you say, and they will know the focus of your heart. King Me or King Jesus?

Can you honestly say, as the psalmist did, "Test me, O LORD, and try me, examine my heart and my mind"?[41] I hope so. Because He *can* see the heart, and He does examine all your thoughts. He loves you and His purpose in your life is to refine you. He reveals what needs to be changed through His Word by His Spirit. He wants you to choose things that bring Him glory. All in all, it is for your good that He sees your heart and tests it, because His desire for you is always and only for your good.

We must always "be careful not to do (our) 'acts of righteousness' before men, to be seen by them. If (we) do, (we) will have no reward from (our) Father in heaven."[42] "For we are his workmanship, created in Christ Jesus for good works, which God prepared beforehand, that we should walk in them."[43] Those works, those deeds—each and every one of them—are to glorify God. Always, my friend, at all times, "whether you eat or drink, or whatever you do, do all to the glory of God."[44]

ALL MEANS MOSTLY ALL ... RIGHT?
So, let me once again ask this: according to 1 Corinthians 10:31, how much of our life is to glorify God? "All" of it! Look again at Colossians 3:17. "And whatever you do, whether in word or deed, do it *all* in the name of the Lord Jesus, giving thanks to God the Father through Him."

Take a moment to focus on the words "whatever" and "all." Do you sense that God isn't giving us the option of leaving anything out? Are you impressed yet with the fact that every aspect of your life should be thought, said, and done in Jesus' name? Is your heart feeling the conviction of the Holy Spirit that you've been so focused on self you have neglected the primary purpose of your life?

Paul is saying that each and every thing you say, as well as each and every thing you do, is to be said and done in the name of Jesus Christ—always with the sole intent of glorifying God. How are you doing with that? Does anyone besides me struggle with this?

It's hard to develop a pattern of life that consistently glorifies our Heavenly Father; hard, but not impossible. To glorify God in *everything* you say and do you must first glorify Him in *everything* you think. Jesus put it this way, "Love the Lord your God with all your heart and with all your soul and with all your strength and with **all your mind**" (Luke 10:27, emphasis mine).

Let me remind you that the foundation we are building our study upon is this: We were created to know God and live godly lives that bring honor and glory to Him in everything we say and do. That is the primary purpose of life, and the way we find true joy.

> Key Thought: *To glorify God in your everyday living you must first glorify Him in your every-moment thinking.*

There is a powerful connection between glorifying God in every thought you think and glorifying Him in every word you say and every deed you do. Tens of thousands of thoughts cross our minds each day. Each one of these thoughts impacts and influences us. Our thoughts, our perceptions, and our assumptions dictate how we react emotionally to an event. Our emotions strongly determine our behaviors.

GIVE IT SOME THOUGHT

1. Why does our concept of God play such an important role in every area of life?

2. As the people who see you daily, and who know you best, are watching you—whom are they seeing (King Me, or God)?

3. Why are all the words you speak (including your attitude and heart's motivation) so important? (See Matthew 12:35-37; Proverbs 10:19; and Ecclesiastes 5:2-3.)

4. Your words expose what is in your heart. Think about your conversations over just the last 24 hours. What do they reveal about the current condition of your heart?

5. According to Jeremiah 17:10—
   a. What does God consider along with your deeds?

   b. Why?

6. Read 1 Samuel 2:3.
   a. What does God do with your deeds?

   b. What does that mean?

7. We saw in 1 Corinthians 10:31 that all of your life is to glorify God.
   a. How much of your life is actually glorifying God *right now*?

   b. What steps are you going to take to improve in this area?

Ask someone you respect and trust to hold you accountable to this.

Endnotes

1. Revelation 1:6; 4:11; 5:12
2. Romans 11:36 (NLT); compare with Romans 16:27; Ephesians 4:21; 1 Timothy 1:17; Jude 25
3. Ecclesiastes 12:13-14
4. 1 Peter 4:11
5. Isaiah 43:7
6. Psalm 86:12; Isaiah 43:7; 1 Corinthians 10:31; Revelation 4:11
7. 1 Corinthians 10:31; compare with Colossians 3:17; Ecclesiastes 12:13
8. Philippians 2:5-8; James 4:7, 10; 1 Peter 5:6-10
9. Psalm 119:30; Luke 6:46; John 14:15, 31; Acts 5:29
10. Isaiah 48:11
11. Isaiah 42:8
12. 2 Timothy 3:16
13. Matthew 5:18
14. Titus 1:2
15. Colossians 4:6
16. Proverbs 10:19
17. Proverbs 12:18
18. Proverbs 13:3
19. Proverbs 15:2
20. Proverbs 15:4
21. Proverbs 16:23-24
22. Proverbs 17:27a
23. Proverbs 17:28
24. Proverbs 21:23
25. Proverbs 25:11
26. For more on this see Matthew 12:36-37; 15:18; Ephesians 4:29; Psalm 19:14; James 1:26.
27. Psalm 139:4
28. Psalm 141:3
29. Psalm 19:14
30. Matthew 12:36 (NIV '84)
31. Matthew 12:34

32. 1 Peter 3:10 (NIV '84)
33. Psalm 71:8 (NIV '84)
34. Psalm 35:28
35. Ecclesiastes 12:14 (emphasis mine)
36. Luke 12:2-3 (NIV '84)
37. Jeremiah 16:17
38. Psalm 90:8
39. Hebrews 4:13 (NIV '84)
40. 1 Corinthians 4:5 (NIV '84)
41. Psalm 26:2 (NIV '84)
42. Matthew 6:1 (NIV '84, additions mine)
43. Ephesians 2:10
44. 1 Corinthians 10:31

> "Woe to those who are wise in their own eyes and clever in their own sight."
> Isaiah 5:21

Five: It's All About ME!

You do know that the title of this chapter isn't true, right? It's *not* about me, and it's not about you. Oh, we often think it is. We can easily believe the lie of the enemy that says, "If I don't look out for myself, who will?" We live under the pretense that it's all about God, but when the rubber meets the road, when the reality of life hits us in the face, we're all about King Me.

As we begin our study this week, let's take a few moments to listen to what God has to say about the title of this chapter.

> "Be not be wise in your own eyes; fear the Lord, and turn away from evil." (Proverbs 3:7)

> "Do you see a man who is wise in his own eyes? There is more hope for a fool than for him." (Proverbs 26:12)

> "Whoever trusts in his own mind is a fool, but he who walks in wisdom will be delivered." (Proverbs 28:26)

> "Do you seek great things for yourself? Seek them not." (Jeremiah 45:5)

> "You have trusted in your own wickedness and have said, 'No one sees me.' Your wisdom and knowledge

mislead you when you say to yourself, 'I am, and there is none besides me.' Disaster will come upon you, and you will not know how to conjure it away. A calamity will fall upon you that you cannot ward off with a ransom; a catastrophe you cannot force will suddenly come upon you." (Isaiah 47:10-11, NIV '84)

❏ Why do we tend to trust more in ourselves than we do God?

> **Key Thought:** *When King Me is sitting high on the throne of your heart, three things happen simultaneously: 1) you will worship King Me; 2) you will expect others to worship King Me; and 3) you will expect God to worship King Me.*

"I" — THE CENTER OF SIN

Have you ever sinned? Silly question, right? After all, every one of us have sinned.[1] Solomon wrote in Ecclesiastes 7:20 that "there is not a righteous man on earth who does good and never sins." Psalm 14:3 tells us, "There is no one who does good, not even one."[2]

There are two things I want you to notice here. First, in both of those verses, God says that no one does good. Let me repeat: No one "does good." The verb "to do" refers to producing something completely on your own. *You* are the one who is performing the action. *You* are accomplishing the task in your own strength and ability.

Second, the word "good" refers specifically to that which is excellent in God's eyes—that which God totally approves. David's point here is that no one, on their own and in their own strength, is capable of producing anything that is excellent in God's eyes. No one does good.

❏ How would you define godliness? What does genuine godliness look like?

❏ What must you do to "be" godly?

We cannot be godly on our own. Only God can be godly. Let me repeat that: only God can be godly!

We are commanded in Scripture to pursue righteousness and godliness.[3] But we must understand that it doesn't come naturally. That is why Paul instructed Timothy to *train* himself to be godly.[4] God loves the one who *pursues* righteousness and godliness.[5] God promises us that when we pursue righteousness, we will be rewarded with life.[6]

We face a monumental problem here. No matter who you are, my friend, no matter where you may be in your walk with God, we all face the same problem. Standing in the way of godliness, hindering personal growth in my relationship with God, preventing God from living out His holiness in my life, is little ol' King Me.

I like pleasure. C'mon, admit it, so do you. I enjoy sin. I'll bet you do, too. It is so bad, but oh, so good! Hebrews 11:25 reminds us that sin has its pleasures "for a season." We give in to sin simply because we enjoy it. We give in to sin because it's easy, effortless, and even comfortable.

Two people have an adulterous relationship because it feels good. A person may gossip because it feels good to have other people look to them as a source of information. It can feel good to explode in anger. Sin does have its pleasures.

At the heart of our struggle for godliness is sin. The heart of sin is "I"—King Me. We all suffer from a worship disorder. Who is sitting on the throne of your heart? When it's all about Me, it can never be about God. This is exactly why we need to remove the "I" from LIFE.

IT'S HARVEST TIME!
It's important to point out here that although sin is pleasurable, it lasts for only "a season." Think about that. A season refers to a brief period of time. That explosion of anger may have felt good at the moment, but the feeling of satisfaction is short-lived when compared to the devastation left in its wake. Sexual impurity has its moment of physical elation, but it fades quickly, leaving behind long-lasting ramifications. Eating that third piece of chocolate cake may relieve the stress now, but the toll it takes on your body is long-term.

Living in northern Indiana, we experience a season every year called corn! Every spring the farmers plow their fields, churning up all that fresh, dark soil; and then they plant the seed. As the corn season progresses through the warm summer months, we are able to literally watch the corn grow (I've even been told that on a quiet summer's eve you can actually hear the corn growing). What I've observed is that every year, without fail, the corn has a time of beginning, a time of growing, and then a time of harvest: a season.

God says that our sin has its pleasure "for a season." During that season, the seeds of temptation will be planted in the soil of your heart, and in the heat of the moment your sin will grow. During that time, your sin will yield the fruit of pleasure. But it lasts for only a season—for a short period of time. At the end of that season there will be a harvest. You see, "sin, when it is full-grown, gives birth to death."[7]

Job tells us that "those who plow evil and those who sow trouble reap it."[8] In Proverbs 22:8 we read, "He who sows wickedness reaps trouble."

❏ Write out Galatians 6:7-8.

When we choose to keep King Me on the throne of our heart, yes, we will enjoy a time of "pleasure," but we will also reap the aftereffects. When we daily choose to walk in the Spirit, we will reap the rewards of godliness.

❏ What do you reap when you sow for King Me?

❏ What are some of the rewards of living for Jesus?

○ Now look at your list; check your heart's motivation. Is that list still about King Me?

THE STRUGGLE WITH SIN
Today, the world around us has almost completely rejected the concept of sin. Because mankind refuses to acknowledge it for what it is, they have no true understanding as to why they are the way they are. Everything they do is considered to be a "lifestyle choice." Hardly anything is acknowledged to be sin anymore.

It's no wonder, then, that we struggle so much with living godly lives when the world's wicked philosophy is all around us, permeating almost everything we see and hear—thus influencing how we think and behave.

Back in the mid-1970s there was a famous actor who coined the phrase, "The Devil made me do it!" It was meant to be funny and cute, and it elicited many laughs from the audience, but I believe it truly expresses the mindset of the world today. Man refuses to take responsibility for his sin. It is far easier to blame someone else for our wrong actions.

So, does the Devil make us sin? No. Does God make us sin? Definitely not! God is "a faithful God who does no wrong, upright and just is He."[9] Job cried out, "Far be it from God that he should do wickedness, and from the Almighty that he should do wrong."[10] James declares, "God cannot be tempted with evil, and he himself tempts no one."[11]

If sin doesn't come from the Devil, and it doesn't come from God, where does it come from?

> "The heart is deceitful above all things and desperately sick." (Jeremiah 17:9)

> "Each of you is following the stubbornness of his evil heart instead of obeying me." (Jeremiah 16:12, NIV '84)

At the very core, or heart, of our being is sin. Without Christ, it's part of who we are. Sin comes from within. We are born sinners. It is part of our makeup to sin.[12] Before Christ, our nature is an old nature, ready and willing to sin.

- ❏ Who sins? (No, this is not a trick question.) Consider Galatians 3:22; 1 Kings 8:46; 2 Chronicles 6:36; and Ecclesiastes 7:20. What other verse(s) from Scripture can you give to support your answer?

We understand that everyone sins. God's Word asks the question, "Who can say, 'I have kept my heart pure; I am clean and without sin'?"[13] The answer, of course, is no one. Even the greatest, most "holy" thing you or I may do in this life is nothing more than a filthy rag before a perfectly holy God.[14]

As a child of God, when King Me is sitting high and mighty on the throne of your heart, you are sinning. That sin hinders your communion with God. The day is coming when Jesus will deliver us once and for all not only from the power of sin, but from the presence of sin in our lives. Until that time, we must daily face our sin head-on and deal with it.

I'M BORN OF GOD — PERFECT!

In the next few paragraphs here, we're going to take a journey. This journey is going to stretch your thinking—in a good way. I say this not to scare you, but to prepare you. Make sure you are reading this section when you have some time to focus on what you're reading. Okay? Ready or not, here we go!

> "No one born of God makes a practice of sinning, for God's seed abides in him; and he cannot keep sinning, because he has been born of God." (1 John 3:9)

For the longest time, I would skip over that verse because it didn't make sense to me. I didn't understand it. Every one of us sins every day. We sin in our thought life. We sin in the things we say and the things we do. So how could John say that the born-again believer cannot sin?

Is John saying that as long as I sin, I'm not really born of God? Not at all. The best way to make sense of all this is to break this text down into its smaller parts, closely examine those parts, and then put them back together again to look at the whole picture. We need to take the time, here, to meditate on God's Word.

A PERFECT BIRTH

The first thing I want you to notice is that the phrase, "is born of God," is written in what's called the perfect tense. Therefore, being "born of God" is something that happened in the past. Having been completed in the past, at the moment of your salvation, being born of God never needs to be repeated, ever again. It's the perfect work of God. What a great promise of our eternal security in Christ!

By using the perfect tense, John is saying that the one who is born of God is saved now and forever. It doesn't matter what sins you have committed or ever will commit, Christ died on the cross for *all* of them. Not a single sin has ever taken or ever will take God by surprise. You will never hear God say to you, "Oh, I didn't know you were going to do that. Sorry—your salvation has been revoked."

Praise God, our salvation is entirely dependent upon an Omniscient and Sovereign God and not on our own efforts! As Paul says in Titus 3:5, it's not by works of righteousness that you or I have done, but according to His mercy that He saved us!

Are you tracking with me here? Watch this next point. That phrase, "is born of God," is also written in what's called the passive voice. That means that it is being done *to* you, not by you. You cannot save yourself. God did it entirely for you. It is His amazing gift of grace and love to you.[15]

So, the first thing we need to understand about 1 John 3:9 is that every born-again believer is *born of God*, once and for all. God accomplished it by His powerful will. You had nothing to do with it, so you cannot lose your salvation. It's not yours. It's God's, and He has chosen freely to give it to you!

NO PRACTICE ALLOWED
Next, notice that John says, "no one...makes a practice of sinning." This is the point where many of us become confused. Look at this verse in the King James Version:
> "Whosoever is born of God doth not commit sin; for His seed remaineth in him; and he cannot sin, because he is born of God." (I John 3:9)

The reason I want you to see it in that version is because of the word "not" (doth *not* commit sin). In the Greek, the original language of the New Testament, that word expresses a full and direct negation: absolutely not ever! It is a complete and utter impossibility. John is stating that that which is born of God does not *ever* commit sin, because it cannot.

This will all begin to make sense in a moment. John writes this verse using what's called the indicative mood—a statement of fact. In other words, it's indisputable: that which is born of God will not ever sin! You can certainly choose to argue against that point, but you would be wrong.

The key here is understanding just what John is referring to when he talks about "that which is born of God." Because whatever *that* is, that is what is incapable of sinning. John goes on to explain. That which is born of God does not sin because God's "seed" remains in the Christian. It's God's seed that cannot sin, because it's the seed that has been born of God.

THE SEED HAS BEEN SOWN
I know, I know, still confused, right? Well, hold on to your hats, because you're about to be blown away!

That little word "seed" is the key to understanding what John is saying. It is the Greek word *sperma* and refers to that which was directly created by God. Whatever it is that God created, *that* is what cannot sin. So, what did God create that is now within you as a child of God?

> "If anyone is in Christ, he is a **new creation**; the old has passed away; behold the new has come." (2 Corinthians 5:17, emphasis mine)

Okay, the new *what* has come? The new nature that you received the moment of your salvation![16] Remember what Paul said in Galatians 2:20? "I no longer live, but Christ lives in me." The "seed" that John refers to is the new nature that God created and placed within you. That seed "remains" in you till the day God calls you home.

The new nature God created and placed within you is incapable of sinning. It is absolutely impossible for anything that comes from God to be contaminated by sin in any way. Your new nature is without flaw, so that means your new nature cannot sin![17]

THE UGH IN STRUGGLE
I can hear the argument now: "But Steve, I'm definitely a Christian, but I still sin!" Yes, you do—and so do I. The fact is, we still struggle with sin. Here's why: our new nature is being housed in a sin-contaminated, fleshly body. Although the former resident—our old, sinful nature—is dead and gone,[18] we still live in a sin-infested body.

That means that as long as we live and breathe here on Earth, sin will continue to be a problem for us. Our new, holy, sin-free nature is living in the old, nasty, sin-ridden flesh. And oh, what a battle those two are fighting—daily! Your flesh is dead set against the new nature, and the new nature is diametrically opposed to the sinful flesh.[19]

Can you relate? Can you feel the battle raging between your new nature and the old flesh? Did you know that is a proof that you are saved? People without Christ don't have this battle because they don't have the new nature living within them.[20]

This is why it's so important that you grow in Christ. The more you grow in your walk with God, the more the Holy Spirit will dominate your flesh—and the less your flesh will defeat you and hinder the work of the Spirit in your life.

WHERE WERE YOU WHEN THE LIGHTS WENT OUT? AT THE LIGHT SWITCH!
   ❏ Write out 1 John 1:5.

God is Light. God is absolutely, totally and completely holy and pure. No darkness, no sin, no evil can exist in God's presence. The brilliance of His light cannot tolerate it.[21] Since no sin at all can exist in His light, we must understand that even though we are born-again, our sin still creates a barrier between us and the absolute purity and holiness of God.

> "But if we walk in the light, as he is in the light, we have fellowship with one another, and the blood of Jesus his Son, cleanses us from all sin." (1 John 1:7)

To enjoy amazing fellowship with the Almighty Creator of the Universe, to experience the incredible joy that being in His presence brings, we have to walk in His light. The problem: when King Me is sitting on the throne, we prefer the darkness.

Have you ever been in a room that is pitch black? I've had times when, as I'm heading to bed, I turn out the lights and immediately I'm "blind." I stand there frozen, hesitant to take a step lest I ram my big toe into a piece of furniture or something else I forgot was there. However, stand there long enough and your eyes begin to adjust. Given enough time, your eyes can "see" in the darkness and you begin to move about the room in greater confidence.

All too often that's how we deal with sin in our lives. We hang around in the darkness long enough that we begin to adjust to our sinful surroundings. We feel comfortable, confident in our behavior. It's less of a "problem." Soon it's not this ugly sin anymore. In fact, it looks pretty good—so, what's the big deal?

DETHRONE AND DEPOSE THE KING
Sin will always—circle it, underline it, highlight it, and put a star by it, *always*—block our fellowship with God. When we claim to be in a right relationship with God, yet allow sin to remain unchecked in our lives, we are living a lie.

We need to come into God's light and stay there. We need to dethrone and depose King Me; leave the darkness of *our* throne room and step into the pure light of God's. Keep in mind that walking in God's light doesn't mean you're living completely without sin. After all, "if we say that we have no sin, we are deceiving ourselves and the truth is not in us."[22]

We're not talking about sinless perfection here. When we are walking in the light, we see our sin the way God sees it. We see our imperfections in the light of His perfectness. Then we are able to properly deal with them. When we stay in the relative darkness of our own throne room, we can't see the things that are in the way of a deeper relationship with God.
❑ What are some ways you can "walk in God's light?"

We need to rise from the throne, walk across the royal chamber of our heart, open wide the door, and let the purity of God's light shine into the darkness. Bow humbly before the King of kings and allow Him to sit on the throne you just abdicated.

The bottom line is this: we have only two choices when it comes to the sin that gets between us and our walk with God. Either we ignore it, denying its existence, covering it up, and face the consequences; or we acknowledge it, confess it, turn our back on it, and enjoy the blessings.

GIVE IT SOME THOUGHT

1. What sin(s) do you tend to give in to? Be honest. Next to each sin, answer this: Why is that a sin (give Scripture to support your answer)?

My Sin: Why it's a sin

2. Look at your list. For each item you identified, answer this: Understanding that this is sin, what am I going to do about it, and when?

My Sin: What I'm going to do about it: When:

3. If King Me remains on the throne of your heart—if you choose to continue in your sin—what are the long-term ramifications?

    a. The impact this will have on my relationship with God is:

    b. The impact this will have upon my relationship with my family is:

    c. The impact this will have upon my relationship with my church family is:

    d. The impact this will have upon my career is:

    e. The impact this will have upon my reputation & testimony to the unsaved is:

Endnotes

1. Romans 3:23
2. Compare with Psalm 14:1; 53:1, 3; Romans 3:12
3. 1 Timothy 6:11; 2 Timothy 2:22
4. 1 Timothy 4:7
5. Proverbs 15:9
6. Proverbs 21:21
7. James 1:15 (NIV '84)
8. Job 4:8 (NIV 1984)
9. Deuteronomy 32:4 (NIV '84)
10. Job 34:10
11. James 1:13
12. Psalm 51:5; Genesis 8:21; Mark 7:21
13. Proverbs 20:9 (NIV '84)
14. Isaiah 64:6
15. Ephesians 2:8
16. See Ephesians 4:24; Colossians 3:10; 2 Corinthians 4:16; Romans 6:6
17. Ephesians 4:24
18. Romans 6:6
19. Galatians 5:17; compare with Romans 7:15-25
20. Romans 8:9
21. Exodus 19:21-24
22. 1 John 1:8

> "Do not conform any longer to the pattern of this world, but be transformed by the renewing of your mind."
> Romans 12:2

Six: Unmasked

Hey, it's downright tough being godly in an ungodly world—agreed? Daily we are slammed with temptation. Around every corner lurks an opportunity to sin. Let's face it: glorifying God in *every* aspect of our lives can sometimes feel like nothing more than a pipe dream.

❏ Write out Galatians 5:16.

As Christians, we are to live by (or walk by) the Spirit. But what does that really mean? How do we faithfully execute that command? How do we consistently live holy lives of integrity and godliness?

To consistently surrender your life to the leading of the Holy Spirit means you are moment-by-moment choosing to say "no" to the constant cravings of your sinful flesh. It also means you are continuously choosing to say "yes" to the Spirit's rule in your heart and mind. It's a choice.

❏ Write out Genesis 4:7.

Now that you've written out Genesis 4:7, read it out loud. You see, every day—in fact, every moment of every day—you are faced with choices. Although the choices may be many, your options are only two.
- Do I listen to King Me, do what I want to do, and suffer the consequences?
- Or, do I choose to dethrone and depose the King, do what God wants me to do, and enjoy the blessings?

THE CHOICEST CHOICES

Let's take a few minutes here to understand why Genesis 4:7 is so crucial to removing the "I" from LIFE.

First, notice God's use of the word "if." He says, "IF you do what is right," or "IF you do what is not right." That little word "if" is called a conditional clause. It requires a choice on your part—with a consequence attached to the choice. Choose this, and this is what will happen. Choose that, and that is what will happen.

God is telling Cain (and us) that you can choose to do what is right or you can choose to do what is wrong. The choice is yours. It's always yours. You not only have the option, you have the divine power (the God-given ability) to make a choice.

When facing temptation to sin, never forget that the choice is yours. You see, one of the powerful lies of the enemy is, "I have no choice. I can't help myself. I have to do this!" Although those thoughts and feelings are very real, so is the truth that you don't "have to" sin. We sin because we choose to sin.

> Key Thought: *We do what we do because we want what we want. We want what we want because in our hearts we believe what we believe.*

You will see this key thought sprinkled throughout this book in various ways and at various times, because it's vital to understand this principle.

There's an old adage that says, "You can choose your actions, but you cannot choose the consequences." For example, I can choose to jump out of an airplane without a parachute; however I cannot choose whether hitting the ground will kill me or not.

Now consider this: you *can* choose your consequences simply by choosing your actions. Think about that for a moment. I can choose not to die, by choosing not to jump out of a plane without a parachute. That only makes sense. Choose the consequences by choosing the actions.

That's the point of Genesis 4:7. If you choose to do what is right, something will happen. Choice—consequence. If you choose to do what is wrong, something will happen. Choice—consequence.

❑ Complete the table below by filling out the consequence for each action.

Action	Consequence
Rolling around in the mud	
Eating an entire half-gallon of ice cream in one sitting	
Exploding at someone in anger	
Lusting for another person	
Read my Bible daily, talk with God daily	

Every action has a consequence. This is true in the spiritual realm as well as the physical.

> "Don't be misled—you cannot mock the justice of God. You will always harvest what you plant. Those who live only to satisfy their own sinful nature will

harvest decay and death from that sinful nature. But those who live to please the Spirit will harvest everlasting life from the Spirit." (Galatians 6:7-8 NLT)

Too often we are duped into believing that we can think however we want to think, say whatever we want to say, and do whatever we want to do without any serious consequences.

> **Key Thought:** *Every choice has a consequence. If you want good consequences, make good choices!*

HIDING BEHIND A MASK
❏ Write out Matthew 23:27.

Asher was a Pharisee of the first order, and he was proud of his accomplishments. His zeal for the letter of the law, personal piety, and devotion to God were unmatched. He worked hard with his fellow Pharisees at crafting their 248 additional commandments and 365 prohibitions—all to ensure they never came close to breaking God's original ten. He was among the elite, the chosen, the faithful few.

He was excited to go out into public today, wearing all of his robes and tassels and jewelry. Yes, at times it was uncomfortable, but that was nothing when compared to the respect he felt from those he passed. He grimaced as he noticed the tax collector cowering in the shadows; now there was the scum of the earth.

Arriving at the synagogue, Asher stood just outside the entrance at the street corner. Closing his eyes, he raised his face toward heaven and inhaled sharply. Slowly opening one eye slightly, he noticed a small crowd beginning to gather around him, anxious to hear him pray. A smile started to form as he began his prayer.

"God, I thank you that I am not like other people—robbers, evildoers, adulterers." He paused for a moment, savoring the sound of approval emanating from the growing crowd. "In fact, God, I doubly thank you that I am nothing like that filthy tax collector over there." Laughter from the crowd and a few shouts of "Glory!" punctuated his prayer.

As Asher continued his monologue, Jabin the tax collector just bowed his head, tears streaming from his eyes. Wracked with guilt and shame over his sin, Jabin began to pound on his chest. Barely whispering, "God," he cried, "please have mercy on me. I am a rotten sinner and desperately need your forgiveness."

This story, taken from Scripture (see Luke 18:9-14), is a picture of two men. One hid behind a mask, one did not. One, in his pride, pretended to be something he was not—a savior of the sinner. The other, in his humility, exposed himself for what he was—a sinner in need of the Savior.

Many of us are similar to Asher. We wear masks around other Christians—even around the unsaved. At church we look (and sound) like good, Bible-believing, God-fearing, faith-walking Christians. Around non-Christians, like chameleons, we secure our masks in place, so we fit right in with our surroundings.

God commands each of us to "not conform any longer to the pattern of this world, but be transformed by the renewing of our mind."[1] Great verse! Great choice. But what does it mean? How do we live it out every day?

We are not to conform to the pattern of this world. The word "conform" expresses the idea of putting on a mask—pretending to be something you are not. When Christians conform to the pattern of this world, we are choosing to adjust our behavior to imitate the traits or features that are characteristic of the world around us.

❏ Why would any Christian ever want to do that? Why would *you* choose to hide your true identity? Why would *you* want to appear to those around you as something you're not?

Now consider carefully your answer to the above questions. The core of the issue is simply this: King Me is sitting on the throne of your heart. You do what you do because in your heart you want what you want.

Whether you're at work, at school, spending time with friends, or just at home with family, the world can be harsh and cruel. A powerful lie of the enemy is that you should try to act like the world around you so that you can fit in with them. After all, you don't want them to tune you out simply because they see you as some kind of religious nut job, right? How can you possibly witness to them then?

Admit it: it can be very easy to put on a mask when you're around the unsaved, acting like they do, talking like they do, laughing at the things they laugh at. However, when you do, that's a sure-fire sign that King Me is sitting supreme on the throne of your heart.
God's command in Romans 12:2 is crystal clear—don't conform to the pattern of this world. Never. Ever. Don't do the things the world does. Don't put on the mask just so you can fit in. Any time (in fact, every time) you choose to act like the world around you, you are doing so for the self-centered purpose of gaining man's approval.
❏ Write out Galatians 1:10.

Now let me pose to you the same question Paul did. Are you trying to win the approval of men, or of God? I'm asking flat-out—what's the motivation of your heart? Why are you doing what you're doing, going where you're going, and saying what you're saying?

Are you trying to please those around you, or are you trying to please God?

> **Key Thought:** *When I am trying to please others, ultimately I'm really trying to please myself. After all, if I can convince you to like me, I can feel good about me. It's all about King Me.*

CAN YOU SEE WHAT I SEE?

Our aim must be to please God, not man.[2] God knows what your real, deep-in-the-heart motivations are, anyway.[3]

- Fact: He "tests our hearts."[4]
- Fact: He knows not only when you sit and when you rise, He perceives *every thought* you ever think.[5]
- Fact: He knows the *secrets* of your heart.[6]

Never forget that man looks on the outward appearance, but the Lord looks at your heart.[7] It is always about your heart.

> **Key Thought:** *God will never be impressed by what you do, if He's not impressed with why you're doing it.*

It's vital that this next point sinks in. It is critical to your spiritual growth that you not miss this. God can and does see your heart. It is actually for your good that He sees your heart, that He tests it. His desire for you is always and only for your good. He sees who you really are. Because His purpose in your life is to guide you into becoming more like Christ, He convicts you and prompts you to choose only those things that bring Him glory.

Don't conform to the pattern of this world. Don't choose to put on a mask and pretend to be what you're not, just so that you can "enjoy life." Consider this: once you've tasted the goodness of God,[8] everything that the world has to offer pales in comparison.

CAN YOU BE WHAT I AM?

We are also commanded in Scripture to "be imitators of God, as dearly loved children."[9] How are you doing with that? Satan wants you to believe that it's an impossible task. After all, he argues, you're still a sinner. God is perfect and you are not, so why bother trying?

> **Key Thought:** *To imitate God, you must evict King Me and allow the Holy Spirit to live His holiness through you.*

When you choose to conform to the pattern of this world, when you choose to hide your real identity behind a mask, you are sinning—plain and simple. Sin is direct disobedience to God's command.[10] You see, God commands us to remove the mask. His orders are clear: "Do not conform to the evil desires you had when you lived in ignorance. But just as He who called you is holy, so be holy in all you do; for it is written: 'Be holy, because I am holy'."[11]

When you allow yourself to conform to the world's way of thinking and behaving, you are committing spiritual adultery. "Friendship with the world is hatred toward God. Anyone who chooses to be a friend of the world becomes an enemy of God."[12] What choices are you making?

- ❏ Write out 1 Peter 1:15.

- ❏ What does it mean to "be holy"?

- ❏ Consider this concept: "SINLESS"…is that possible for you?

If we're being honest—and we should always be honest—our gut reaction to the above question about being sinless is probably, "No, not possible; I still struggle with sin. I certainly need to strive for it, try my best to achieve it, but it can't be done until I arrive in Heaven." Before you solidly commit to that answer, think hard.

❏ We see that God is "holy"—what does that mean?

You just wrote 1 Peter 1:15 above. Read it again. God's command is clear: you are to be holy, *even as* He is holy. So, holiness (sinlessness) must be within the realm of possibility. But how?

MIRACULOUS METAMORPHOSIS

Our answer is found in Romans 12:2. "Do not conform any longer to the pattern of this world, but be transformed by the renewing of your mind." Instead of conforming, instead of putting on a mask, instead of pretending to be what we're not, instead of trying to please man (thus pleasing ourselves), instead of giving in to sin, we are to *be transformed*.

"Transformed" is an awesome word. In the Greek (the language of the New Testament) it is the word *metamorpho-o*, from which we get our English word "metamorphosis." According to the Merriam-Webster Dictionary, a metamorphosis is a supernatural process whereby something changes from one thing into something totally different from what it used to be. What makes a metamorphosis so unique is that the change takes place *from the inside out*!

The most well-known example of a metamorphosis God has given us is that of a caterpillar to a butterfly. The reason a caterpillar changes into a butterfly is simply because the nature of the butterfly is already *inside* the caterpillar. It's that nature inside that is lived out on the outside.

Imagine that you go to your backyard and dig up a big, juicy, wriggling earthworm. Bringing it inside, you set it on the dining room table (after putting down some newspaper, of course). Next, you cut out a small pair of wings from colored construction paper. Laying the wings on top of the earthworm, you proceed to pin the wings on to the worm. What would you have? A squirming worm, of course, (and a tiny pinhole in your nice dining room table)!

The reason you do not have a butterfly is because it's just not within the nature of the worm to become a butterfly. You tried to make an external change. To become a butterfly, there must first be an internal transformation.

Too often, we try to make *external changes* to our life. We try to "do this" and "not do that," thinking that is what it takes to be holy. We take a crack at our interpretation of "holiness" and "godliness," only to end up discouraged when we fail. This is why, when we see the word "sinless," we think "impossible."

Remember, man looks on the outward appearance. If you're trying to impress man, then go ahead and attempt your external changes. Go ahead and pin "Christian" paper wings on your back. But you'll never be able to fly.

> **Key Thought:** *It's not about what's on the outside, but Who is on the inside.*

Paul says that we are to be transformed. We are to go through a spiritual metamorphosis. As a Christian, your life should be different now from what you were before you were saved. That kind of change can only take place from the inside out.
❑ Read Galatians 2:20. What (who) is on the inside of every Christian?

As a born-again believer, you have a brand new, holy nature created by God Himself *inside* of you. How do we know it's holy? Paul tells us that that new nature was "created after the likeness of God in true righteousness and holiness."[13]

Don't miss this. Don't skim over this truth. This is powerful. God created a new nature, a holy nature, a nature incapable of sinning (a nature just like His)—and He placed that nature inside of you. Then He moved in!

> Key Thought: *Your new nature was created to be "like God" (not god-like, but like God—having the same nature as God). It was created to be truly righteous and truly holy: without sin.*

Your everyday lifestyle should be reflecting your new, holy nature within. The things you say, the things you do, the choices you make are all to be in perfect step with the new nature inside of you. When God commands you to be holy, even as He is holy, it's possible because He put His holiness inside of you! That which is on the inside—your new, holy nature—is lived out when you are transformed.

LET IT GO TO YOUR HEAD
Paul goes on to tell us, in Romans 12:2, that this transformation takes place only as we renew our minds. The only way I can live out God's holiness in my everyday behavior is to change the way I think.

How does renewing my mind bring about a spiritual metamorphosis? How does changing the way I think change the way I live? To answer that question, let's think for a moment about the word "renew." We are transformed when we renew our minds. Paul uses a very special word here, which literally means "to renovate."

Think about it this way. When you renovate a home, you are removing all the old, nasty, rotting, out-of-date items, and replacing it all with brand new finishes, appliances, furniture—the works! That's the word "renew" in Romans 12:2. To live a transformed life, to live out God's holiness in your everyday words and actions, you must first renovate your mind. You need to totally demolish the old thought process and replace it with a brand-new way of thinking.

Removing the "I" from Life

❑ What is the old way of thinking that gets us into trouble?
How can I gratify _____?

❑ What's wrong with that kind of thinking?

When my mind is focused on King Me, every thought, every word, every choice, every decision, every action—all of me—is geared toward one thing: making the King happy, happy, happy. That kind of thinking leads to self-centered, self-worshiping behavior. That mindset needs to be totally gutted and replaced with a new way of thinking.

❑ What is the new way of thinking we need to put into our minds?
How can I glorify _____?

❑ When your mind is totally focused on how to glorify God, what will your words, choices, and actions be like?

CONSTRUCTION ZONE AHEAD
If you've ever tried your hand at renovation, you know that it's best to have a good set of tools at your disposal. They make the job go easier and faster. God has given you an effective and powerful tool that enables you to renovate your mind. It's called the Bible.

In John 17:17 Jesus is praying for his disciples, which includes you and me. In that prayer, He asks God to "sanctify them by the truth, your word is truth." To paraphrase, Jesus is saying, "Father, make your children holy," (remember, we're commanded to be holy), "and set them apart from sin. Your absolute truth, which is found only in your Word, is the tool that will help them obey your command."

> **Key Thought:** *As you open God's Word and daily read His truth, the Holy Spirit is working. He is using the tool of Scripture to renovate your mind, changing the way you think.*

If you allow yourself the momentary thought of how you can fulfill the sinful desires of your flesh, your life will begin to alter course. You will begin to focus more and more upon the goal of meeting that desire.

❑ Write out Romans 13:14.

Remember, when you live by the Spirit, you will not gratify the desires of the flesh.[14] Praise God we have the Holy Spirit dwelling within us! Jesus gave us this wonderful promise: "When the Spirit of truth comes, he will guide you into all truth, for he will not speak on his own authority, but whatever he hears he will speak, and he will declare to you the things that are to come. He will glorify me, for he will take what is mine and declare it to you."[15]

Every time you open your Bible, every time you study God's Word, the Holy Spirit is right there inside you, helping you understand what God is saying. He guides you in applying God's truth to your life. Then, as you follow His leading, as you apply the Word of God to your life, you will be living by the Spirit. The end result? You will not gratify the desires of the flesh!

Removing the "I" from Life

REMOVE THE MASK!

Take off your mask and live a transformed life! Change, real lasting change, is not only possible, but it is God's promise to you as you choose daily to yield to the leading of the Holy Spirit.

As the Spirit teaches you and guides you deeper into God's Word, and as you let the Word of God wash over you—saturating your mind with His truth—you will begin to renovate your thinking. This in turn will result in a drastic change in your behavior. Why? Because you've dethroned and deposed King Me, and have allowed God to take His rightful place.

GIVE IT SOME THOUGHT

- How does renewing your mind bring about a transformation that changes you from the inside out?

- What good does the Bible do you if it just sits on the shelf? Explain your answer.

- Read John 14:26. One ministry of the Holy Spirit in your life is to remind you of what God has said to you. In order for that to happen (for you to *remember* God's Word), what must you do first?

Endnotes
1. Romans 12:2 (NIV '84)
2. See 2 Corinthians 5:9-11; Acts 5:29
3. 1 Chronicles 28:9
4. 1 Thessalonians 2:4
5. Psalm 139:1-2
6. Psalm 44:21
7. 1 Samuel 16:7
8. Hebrews 6:5; 1 Peter 2:3
9. Ephesians 5:1
10. 1 John 3:4
11. 1 Peter 1:14-16 (NIV '84)
12. James 4:4 (NIV '84)
13. Ephesians 4:24
14. Galatians 5:16
15. John 16:13-14; compare with John 16:5-12

> "Has the Lord as great delight in burnt offerings and sacrifices, as in obeying the voice of the Lord? Behold, to obey is better than sacrifice, and to listen than the fat of rams."
> 1 Samuel 15:22

Seven: Saved to Sit-Soak-and-Sour... NOT!

If you were to look closely at my thumb—right or left, it doesn't really matter—you would not see even a hint of green to it (except for maybe the time I hit it with the hammer). If I want something to grow in my garden, I typically go to the nearest gardening supply store and pick up a handy-dandy bottle of stuff to sprinkle on my plants. Voilà—they grow—it's a miracle!

Why can't I do that with my spiritual life? It feels like I'm constantly growing the weeds of sin instead of the fruit of righteousness. Wouldn't it be great if we could just go to church on Sunday, have the pastor sprinkle some Spiritual Miracle Grow onto our hearts, and voilà, we mature and produce godliness?

BACK TO THE BASICS
- ❏ I have a very basic question for you. Are you a Christian? Are you a born-again believer?

If your answer to the above question is something like this: "Yes, I've put my faith and trust in the finished work of Christ on Calvary," then, according to God's promise in His word you are saved! You will be in Heaven for eternity—not because of anything good that you have done, but because of all that God has already done on your behalf.

> "For by grace you have been saved through faith. And this is not your own doing; it is the gift of God, not a result of works, so that no one may boast. For we are his workmanship, created in Christ Jesus for good works, which God prepared beforehand, that we should walk in them." (Ephesians 2:8-10)

In the passage above, please circle the words "not a result of works." Paul is telling us that it's not by our own personal efforts at godliness that we are saved. No matter how many good, great, and grand "Christian" deeds you do in your lifetime, you can never merit Heaven on your own. God expects absolute perfection—something we cannot achieve.

> "Not everyone who says to me 'Lord, Lord,' will enter the kingdom of heaven, but only he who does the will of my Father who is in heaven." (Matthew 7:21, NIV '84)

Look at the last part of that verse carefully. Doesn't Jesus say right here that to enter the kingdom of Heaven you have to DO the will of God? Isn't that doing good works to be worthy of Heaven? After all, Jesus Himself said I have to "do" something to enter His kingdom. Right?

Stay with me, here. On the surface it might appear that way, but any time you study God's Word you must always compare Scripture with other Scripture. Otherwise you run the high risk of misunderstanding and misinterpreting what God is saying.

We just read in Ephesians 2:8-9 that we are saved by *God's amazing grace*, not by our faulty works and futile efforts. Paul tells us that we "are justified freely by his grace through the redemption that came by Christ Jesus."[1] He also said that God "has saved us and called us to a holy life—not because of anything we have done but because of his own purpose and grace."[2]

- ❑ When you make salvation all about works—or even partially about works—who is sitting on the throne of your heart, and why?

- ❑ What if Jesus did 98% of the work of salvation for you, but you have to do the remaining 2%?

- ❑ Read Isaiah 64:6 and Ecclesiastes 7:20. Why can't I gain access into Heaven based on how good I am?

Jesus said, "On that day many will say to me, 'Lord, Lord, did we not prophesy in your name, and cast out demons in your name, and do many mighty works in your name?"[3] It sure sounds like the people Jesus is describing here were doing things that fit into the category of God's will. After all, they prophesied in His name. They drove out the enemy. They performed miracles! Doesn't God want us to do mighty things in His name?

Yet Jesus goes on to say:
"Then I will tell them plainly, 'I never knew you. Away from me, you evildoers!'" (Matthew 7:23)

Their eternal destiny didn't rely on *their ability* to do good deeds, even if they did them in the name of the Lord. Their hope—your hope and my hope—for eternity rests solely on something else—Someone else.

In the verse above (Matthew 7:23), please underline the words "I never knew you." You see, "The Lord knows those who are his."[4] Jesus said that God "calls his own sheep by name."[5] Look once again at Matthew 7:23. Jesus didn't know them. They were doing good deeds in His name, but He didn't *know* them. In fact, He calls them "evildoers" (literally, breakers of His laws).

> "Not everyone who says to me 'Lord, Lord,' will enter the kingdom of heaven, but the one who does the will of my Father who is in heaven." (Matthew 7:21)

The reason I've repeated this verse here is so I can draw your attention to the phrase "does the will of my Father." Jesus clearly states that the *only* way to get into Heaven is by doing something—a specific something—that God expects you to do. He has a definite will, and you must do that particular thing in order to get into Heaven. That is the only way He will let you spend an eternity with Him.

❑ Read John 3:14-18. Then, write out John 3:36.

❑ According to the verses above, what is God's specific will? What must you (or anyone on planet Earth) do in order to get into Heaven?

Do you remember what Jesus said in Matthew 7:21? "Only he who does the will of my Father who is in heaven" will enter the kingdom of Heaven.

> "For **my Father's will is** that everyone who looks to the Son and believes in him shall have eternal life." (John 6:40, NIV '84, emphasis mine)

Again, I ask: have you done that?

FORMED TO FUNCTION

This book is all about how to remove the "I" from life—dethroning and deposing King Me. So why a section on salvation? After all, an assumption I am making here is that you already know Christ as your Savior. You've already placed your faith in Jesus and believe with all your heart that He died in your place, took the penalty for your sin upon Himself, and that your sin-debt is now paid in full. So why devote even a part of this book to the subject?

❑ Removing the "I" from life begins by understanding the true purpose of your salvation. Why did Jesus die on the cross for you? Why did He save you? (Hint: it's more than just to save you from your sin.)

Paul asks a very interesting question of the Christians in Galatia that helps emphasize my point here.

> "You foolish Galatians! Who has bewitched you? Before your very eyes Jesus Christ was clearly portrayed as crucified. I would like to learn just one thing from you: Did you receive the Spirit by observing the law, or by believing what you heard? Are you so foolish? After beginning with the Spirit, are you now trying to attain your goal by human effort?" (Galatians 3:1-3, NIV '84)

That question is worthy of our consideration. We know from Scripture that it is by God's grace we are saved, not by works.[6] We understand that our faith in Christ is the key.[7] But when King Me is sitting on the throne of my heart, I begin to make salvation all about me instead of God.

❑ What are some ways we make salvation about us? (e.g., I'm saved from an eternity in Hell.)

> "For by grace you have been saved through faith. And this is not your own doing; it is the gift of God, not a result of works, so that no one may boast. For we are his workmanship, created in Christ Jesus for good works, which God prepared beforehand, that we should walk in them." (Ephesians 2:8-10)

Please note in the verse above the words "we are God's workmanship." In fact, go ahead and underline them. God created you with a specific purpose in mind. He designed you with great care and effort, because He has a plan for your life. You are His workmanship.

What is that plan? What is God's purpose for your life? Are you saved to just sit, soak, and sour? No way! In short, He saved you "for good works, which God prepared beforehand, that we should walk in them" (Ephesians 2:10).

> **Key Thought:** *You aren't saved by your good works, but you are saved to do good works.*

Once you have become a new creation,[8] God expects you to grow in your spiritual life and do "good works" for His glory.

> "So, whether you eat or drink, or whatever you do,
> do all to the glory of God." (1 Corinthians 10:31)

Jesus commands us to let our "light shine before men, that they may see your good deeds and glorify your Father in Heaven."[9] God's Word instructs us "how to live in order to please God."[10]

We've been formed to function. Designed to declare. Made to magnify. Prepared to perform in a way that brings others to Christ. God wants you to do good works.

YES, M'LORD
Let me draw your attention to the fact that we are to "live" in a way that pleases God.

❑ Write out James 1:22.

I must give you a very serious warning here, so sit up and take notice. Here it is: As you read God's Word, you are going to learn God's truth. However, the truths you will discover from the Bible will do you absolutely no good.

Yes, you read that right. No, I'm not a heretic. No, I'm not spouting false truths. It's a fact. The truths in the Bible are worthless to you IF they are not put into practice. Living a godly life that consistently glorifies our Heavenly Father happens only when you *do* the truth. Don't just read it. Don't just listen to it. Don't even talk it. Do it!

Paul charged young Timothy to "correctly handle the word of truth."[11] Correct handling of God's Word begins with reading it, sure. It certainly includes listening to it. But if that's all you do, you have failed in the charge. You are not "correctly" handling it. In fact, you're mishandling it. Only when you take that truth and apply it to your daily life are you correctly handling it.

> "Do not merely listen to the word and so deceive yourselves. Do what it says. Anyone who listens to the word but does not do what it says is like a man who looks at his face in a mirror and, after looking at himself, goes away and immediately forgets what he looks like. But the man who looks intently into the perfect law that gives freedom, and continues to do this, not forgetting what he has heard, but doing it—he will be blessed in what he does." (James 1:22-25, NIV '84)

❑ What does it mean to "be deceived"?

❑ In what way can merely listening to God's Word deceive you?

My friend, NEVER let God's Word go in one ear and out the other. When you "merely listen" to Scripture, you're hearing the words—considering what they are saying, for a moment—then promptly dismissing them as irrelevant to you and your situation.

THE DECEPTION CONNECTION
When you choose to merely listen to God's Word, when you choose to do nothing about what you've heard, God says you *will* be deceived.

To deceive means to lie to; to cause someone to believe something that is untrue. Never forget that God's Word is absolute truth, and no lie ever comes from God's truth.[12] What James is warning us about is this: just *hearing* the Word of God, taking a moment to consider what God is saying, then choosing to dismiss it as irrelevant causes you to be deceived.

When you choose to ignore the Holy Spirit's prompting in your life, choosing to believe, "I've got this," and "That doesn't really apply to me," you are deceived. You are duped by the enemy into believing something that is untrue.

Every time you sit in a Sunday service and listen to the sermon, every time you attend your Bible fellowship or Sunday School class and hear a lesson taught, every time you go to small group Bible study, every time you have your personal devotions or turn on the radio to hear your favorite preacher—every time—you are listening to the Word of God. Are God's words "going in one ear and out the other"?

What you do with what the Holy Spirit reveals to you is critical at this point. If you are not applying to your life what God is showing you, then you are *merely listening,* and God says you are being deceived.

Let me repeat this point. Let the Holy Spirit drill this into your long-term memory bank. We must not "merely listen" to God's Word and then go merrily on our way, choosing to do nothing about it.

> **Key Thought:** *If you think you can ignore God's Word, if you believe that you'll apply it to your life "later," you're believing a lie.*

Mirror, Mirror in My Hand

Once again, take a moment to read what James says:

> "Do not merely listen to the word and so deceive yourselves. Do what it says. Anyone who listens to the word but does not do what it says is like a man who looks at his face in a mirror and, after looking at himself, goes away and immediately forgets what he looks like. But the man who looks intently into the perfect law that gives freedom, and continues to do this, not forgetting what he has heard, but doing it—he will be blessed in what he does." (James 1:22-25, NIV '84)

Have you ever looked in the mirror and noticed your hair all messed up or a glowing red zit strategically stationed on the end of your nose? What do you do about it? Do you shrug your shoulders thinking, "Eh, no biggie," and walk away having done nothing about it? Of course not.

In James' example, that person has seen in the mirror of God's Word that a problem exists. He acknowledges it's there. He fully understands there's a problem that needs to be dealt with. Yet, for some unknown reason, he makes the choice not to deal with it right there and then. He goes on his way, fully intending to take care of the problem—later. The funny thing is, "later" rarely comes. Other things such as the everyday activities, pressures, and demands of life capture his attention.

The result? He forgets the problem is there and so doesn't deal with it. By not dealing with it right then, he runs the risk of it growing into an even bigger problem. By not addressing it when the Holy Spirit revealed it to him, he risks developing a hard heart toward that issue and never dealing with it at all.

Don't misunderstand. He takes the time to consider it. He agrees with God that it's an issue in his life that needs to be dealt with. But it just isn't as important right now as _____ (fill in the blank with whatever else is crying out for your attention). So, instead of addressing the issue, he chooses to walk away. And because the issues of life are all around him, he promptly forgets what the mirror has revealed to him.

Result: He was deceived. He came to a wrong conclusion, which is proven by his lack of action.

❏ When you are aware of a wound on your body and choose to do nothing about it, what are the potential ramifications?

❏ When God reveals an area of your life that needs addressing, and you choose not to attend to it, what are the potential ramifications?

Just like an open sore, left unattended it will fester and grow. It will become larger and harder to deal with later. It is vital that you face head-on whatever God reveals to you. Whatever it may be, don't wait!

James speaks of the man who *looks* at his face in a mirror and, after *looking* at himself, goes away and immediately forgets what he looks like.[13] The verb "look" means to perceive, to observe in such a way that you understand what you're looking at. You are considering the thing you're looking at so attentively that you are *fixing your gaze* upon it. You see the problem that God is pointing out. You are fully aware it's there.

ACTION IS THE KEY; DO IT IMMEDIATELY

I think it's fairly safe to say that if you looked in the mirror and saw a big zit glowing at the end of your nose, you would immediately address the issue. It wouldn't even cross your mind to walk away until it was dealt with. The man James is talking about sees something much more severe than a little spot of acne, yet he still turns and walks away without dealing with it.

> **Key Thought:** *The trouble lies not in the identification of the problem but in the execution of the solution.*

In verse 24 James points out that the moment that man walks away from the mirror, he "immediately forgets what he looks like." James uses a very specific word for "forget." It's a word that means you are intentionally neglecting something. You no longer care for it.

Now take a moment and think about that. The fact that he *no longer* cares for it suggest that at one point he did care. However, something else came in and drew his attention away from the problem. He then chose to focus on it instead of the problem that was revealed to him. By putting his attention on that other thing, he began to care more for that than for the imperfection he saw in the mirror.

❏ What things in life tend to draw your attention away from God and His Word?

It's important to note that although James says this man no longer cared for the problem, he's not saying that it was unimportant to him. This man didn't look in the mirror, see his problem, and say, "Eh, no big deal." It's not that he didn't care *about* it, but that he didn't take the time right then and there to care *for* it—to attend to it. Action is the key. Do it now; don't delay!

When you read your Bible, and the Holy Spirit reveals an area of your life He wants you to work on, I'm sure you don't shrug your shoulders and say, "No biggie." You agree with Him that it's something you need to take care of. But if you don't care for it right then and there, you're coming to a wrong conclusion. That is how merely listening to the Word can deceive you.

When God speaks to you, please don't just walk away. I urge you to deal with it right then and there. Whatever appointment you may need to keep, whatever thing you are planning to do, whatever show is on TV that you're dying to watch, it can wait! In the whole scheme of things, they pale in importance compared to the high priority of having your heart right with God. Don't chance it. Don't risk walking away from the mirror and forgetting what God showed you in His Word. Later may be too late.

LEAN IN
> "The man who looks intently into the perfect law that gives freedom, and continues to do this, not forgetting what he has heard, but doing it—he will be blessed in what he does." (James 1:25, NIV '84)

In the verse above, please circle the words "looks intently." We are to look intently into God's Word. James isn't talking about casually glancing at Scripture. He's not referring to a brief "devotional." That phrase refers to stooping forward, leaning into a thing in order to look at it closely.

Just picture looking at yourself in a mirror. You notice something on the end of your nose. You lean forward, getting as close to the mirror as you can so you can see it better. The closer you get, the better you can identify what it is and deal with the problem.

When you're looking intently into Scripture, you're leaning in so that you can look closely at what God is revealing to you. You are making the time to dig into God's Word, comparing Scripture with Scripture, reading commentaries, talking with godly Christians, all for the purpose of discovering what God wants you to do about it. You're dealing with the problem.

Have you ever stood in front of a mirror with the lights out? What did you see? Silly question, right? You don't stand in a darkened room to look in the mirror; you turn on a light. Without the light, you cannot see the problem—you cannot properly deal with it.

Not only is God's Word a mirror, it's also a *lamp* to our feet and a *light* to our path.[14] Think about that. God's commands are a lamp, His teaching is light.[15] Every time you open the Bible, every time you read the Scriptures, every time you are exposed to God's truth, you are coming into the light.[16] That light will expose, as if in a mirror, the issues you need to deal with.[17]

APPLY DAILY

Let's say that you bump your chin on something and it begins to bleed. You go to the bathroom and step in front of the mirror. Why? You want to see what's causing the pain and how to deal with it. Leaning forward, you notice an open wound. What are you going to do about it?

You would open the medicine cabinet, grab some ointment and a Band-Aid. You then wash off your chin, gently dry it, apply the ointment, and put on the bandage. Over the next few days you periodically look in the mirror to see how it's doing. You clean it again, putting on more ointment and a fresh bandage. You continue to do this daily until the wound is healed.

Addressing your spiritual blemish requires more than just confessing it to God. It involves going to the Word of God and finding the truths in Scripture that apply to that issue in your life. Study it, memorize it, meditate on those truths, and *choose to live them out* in your everyday life in such a way that you never accommodate that sin again.

God has so much He wants to show you in His Word. Within the pages of Scripture you will find God's truth about who you are, who He is, and how you are to live that life of integrity and godliness you are seeking.

At times that means His Word is going to show you things that need to be dealt with: maybe a nagging sin that needs to be removed; or an attitude that needs to be changed; or a thought-process that needs some adjusting. Other times He just wants to show you His amazing grace, mercy, and love. In either case, a cursory glance at the Bible will not reveal to you the depths of His truth. It's only when you look intently into His Word that you will see your true reflection.

SAVED TO SIT, SOAK, AND BE SQUEEZED
Think about a big, yellow sponge—the kind you use to wash your car. In one hand you hold the sponge, in the other a bucket of water. The sponge is dry. The water is wet. Placing the sponge into the bucket of water, what happens to the sponge? It begins to soak up the water around it.

Once the sponge is full, it sinks to the bottom of the bucket. It cannot soak up any more water. In order for that sponge to absorb more water, what must be done to that sponge? Squeeze it, of course. Wring it hard to force out the water that's in it. Then, place it back into the bucket of water, where it's able to soak in more.

That's what God expects of you. You're that sponge. Read God's Word. Soak in all of the truth that you can. But understand, God doesn't want you to sit, soak, and stay there. Never are we to sit, soak, and sour.

God will allow situations in your life that will wring that truth out of you. Every test, every trial, every situation you find yourself in, God is bringing into your life so that you can live out the truths you have absorbed.

Each day of your life will bring new things. Each day of your life you will discover ways in which the things you're learning from God's Word can be lived out that day. What are you going to do with them?

GIVE IT SOME THOUGHT

- ❏ James uses the words "do" and "doer" (James 1:22, 23). They carry the idea that you are putting in the required effort to apply God's truth to your daily life. What steps must you take to actually "do" God's Word?

- ❏ When you look in the mirror and see a blemish on your face, you stop and deal with it. Why do we tend not to do the same thing when we look into the mirror of God's Word and see an issue in our life?

- ❏ When God reveals an area of your life that needs addressing, and you choose not to attend to it immediately, you risk that area getting worse. What area(s) in *your* life does God want to address that you've been avoiding?

Endnotes
1. Romans 3:24 (NIV '84)
2. 2 Timothy 1:9 (NIV '84)
3. Matthew 7:22
4. 2 Timothy 2:19
5. John 10:3
6. Ephesians 2:9; Galatians 2:16
7. Acts 16:31; 1 Corinthians 1:21; Ephesians 2:8; Romans 10:9
8. 2 Corinthians 5:17
9. Matthew 5:16 (NIV '84)
10. 1 Thessalonians 4:1 (NIV '84)
11. 2 timothy 2:15 (NIV '84)
12. 1 John 2:21
13. James 1:23-24
14. Psalm 119:105
15. Proverbs 6:23
16. John 3:21
17. Ephesians 5:13-14

> "Man shall not live by bread alone, but by every word that comes from the mouth of God."
> Matthew 4:4

EIGHT: TIME TO EAT!

When you read God's Word, when you invest the time to pore over its pages and dig into its storehouse to discover the buried treasure within, you will find that King Me begins to feel quite uncomfortable sitting on the throne of your heart. You realize just how hungry for God you really are.

> **Key Thought:** *A great way to dethrone and depose King Me is to open your Bible daily and fill your heart with the truths of God's Word.*

All the sinful pleasures you've been pursuing, all those things you assumed would fill and fulfill you, everything you thought looked and smelled like a big, juicy T-bone steak, ends up being a bunch of mushed leftovers stuffed into a pig's intestine (my definition of a hot dog). It leaves you empty, dissatisfied and starving.

❑ Write out Matthew 4:4.

> "Your words were found, and I ate them, and your words became to me a joy and the delight of my heart." (Jeremiah 15:16)

Removing the "I" from Life

> "How sweet are your words to my taste, sweeter than honey to my mouth." (Psalm 119:103)

FOOD FIT FOR A KING
How fulfilling would it be to sit down to a banquet, with all manner of mouth-watering, delectable choices of food placed in front of you, only to sit there and stare at it? How satisfying would it be to look at the food, talk about the food, smell the food, but never once consume the food? That would be silly, right?

Unfortunately, many Christians today are spiritually starving even though God has provided them with an amazing banquet of truth from His Word.
  ❏ Write out Psalm 119:97.

King David was a man who truly loved the Word of God. He saw Scripture as a meal to be consumed—food fit for a king. In fact, he said that the one who experiences genuine happiness is the one "whose delight is in the law of the LORD, and on his law meditates day and night."[1]
  ❏ So how are you doing with that? Do you *love* reading your Bible? Do you *delight* in studying God's Word? Do you meditate on it daily?

  ❏ If "yes"—why? If "no"—why not?

To experience the kind of happiness David is talking about—to be truly blessed of God—we need to "delight" in God's Word. A person who is "delighting" in God's Word is finding great pleasure in it—to the point of longing for it constantly.

❑ Read Psalm 1:1-3. According to verse two, what word describes how the one feels who is in God's Word day and night?

❑ According to verse one, when you delight in God's Word, what are your choices and actions like?

❑ According to verse three, what's the result of delighting in God's Word?

Please note the fact that God doesn't say that the one who *appreciates* His Word, or the one who *respects* His Word will be like a tree, yielding fruit and prospering. He doesn't say that anyone who brings a Bible to church and does daily devotions is the one who will be blessed. It's the one who *delights* in God's Word and *meditates* on it daily. Are you that person? Do you want to be?

DELIGHT IN THE LIGHT
God's Word reveals God's heart, and it's His heart that will capture you!

❑ Write out Psalm 112:1.

My friend, you should long for the time each day when you can sit down with your Bible and listen to your Father speak His heart to you. Every day you should be anxiously looking forward to the moment when you can open Scripture and cling to your Father's every word.

❑ Why do most Christians struggle with this? Why do we tend to feel the opposite regarding reading our Bible?

How we see our Bible makes all the difference in the world. If we see God's Word as irrelevant or boring, if we see it as cumbersome and a chore to be done by "good Christians," we will be hesitant to spend time in it. We will choose to put off reading it as long as we can, in favor of other things we perceive to be more enjoyable and relaxing. Then, when we do pick up our Bible to read it, we're doing it more out of a sense of duty than to develop a deeper relationship with the Father.

However, when we see Scripture for what it really is—God speaking to us, telling us how much He loves us, giving us a glimpse into who He is and all He has planned for us; when you understand that it is God sitting down with you to share His heart with you—you become anxious to invest your time drawing closer to the One who loves you so much.

> **Key thought:** *The Bible is God's Word to you, not to be read and understood, but to be eaten and digested.*[2]

A Personal Touch

"Direct me in the path of your commands, for there I find delight…I delight in your commands because I love them…if your law had not been my delight, I would have perished in my affliction." (Psalm 119:35, 47, 92, NIV '84)

This truth became very real to me a few years ago. There was a time in my life when I turned my back completely on my family—and on God. I chose to pursue the pleasures of sin for a season. I chose to set King Me high on the throne of my heart and let Me reign supreme.

During those dark days, God led a guy named Roger into my life. Roger began taking me deep into the Bible. We met weekly, investing our time in seeing what God had to say about how He loved me just as I was. I discovered what God's grace, His mercy, His forgiveness, and His never-ending love was all about.

Each week I was challenged to read my Bible daily, and I was given Scripture verses to memorize. Every time I opened my Bible, every moment I invested in studying God's Word, the Holy Spirit was awakening within me a deeper desire to know God more. I began to feel a hunger—a craving for more. I began to relish every second I could devote to reading, hearing my Father speak to me, heart-to-heart.

You see, when I began digging into the Word of God, studying the Scriptures, meditating on them, memorizing them, and talking about them with my accountability partners, that is when true change started happening in my heart. Digging deep into God's Word and getting to know God more required determined action on my part. No one else could do it for me—it was personal. If it was going to happen, I had to choose to do it.

Today I am more excited about the Word of God than ever before. I am passionate about reading God's truth and hiding His principles in my heart. I am humbled every time the Holy Spirit shows me another truth and teaches me yet another lesson.

> "If your law had not been my delight, I would have perished in my affliction."[3]

Had I not begun to dig into my Bible, had I not started studying, memorizing, meditating upon and seeking to apply God's Word to my life—had I not delighted in God's Word, I would still be gripped by my sin. I would be perishing because of my own self-centered, egotistical, King Me attitude.

God's Value Meal

Some fast food restaurants offer what's often called a "value meal." It's simply a grouping of items on a menu that are offered together at a lower price than they would cost if you purchased each item individually. All too often that's how we approach the Word of God. We see Church as a "fast food restaurant" where we can take in a dash of worship songs, a large helping of Bible teaching, and a side of fellowship—all for the price of an hour on Sunday with a couple of dollars put in the offering plate.

Reading God's Word is never to be treated as a value meal. It is, however, a meal full of great value.
- ❏ Write out 1 Peter 2:2.

Pause for a moment and consider what you just wrote down. What milk is to a baby, the Word of God is to your soul. It's the food that nourishes you spiritually. But you have to eat! Listen carefully here—we're not talking about an occasional snack on God's Word. This isn't a one-day, Sunday thing.

Think about it this way: a baby has a passion for milk that will not rest until his hunger is satisfied. When a baby wants to eat, nothing else matters. The world as we know it comes to a screeching halt until baby is fed. Baby doesn't care whether or not you have to set aside your priorities. He doesn't care if mama is exhausted. The time of day (or night) means nothing to him when he's hungry. The fact is, when it's time to eat—it's time to eat!

Is that how you see God's Word? Do you hunger for it the way a baby hungers for its milk? Do you come to the point each day when you want to feed on Scripture and nothing else matters?

There are times when a mother tries to pacify her baby with fake food. You've seen it. Baby is crying, mama isn't ready to feed him yet, so she sticks a pacifier in his mouth. Voilà! Baby is quiet—for the moment. At some point, he begins to wise up to the fact that what he's sucking on isn't producing the desired effect. That's when he spits out the fake and screams out, "I want the real thing, and I want it now!"

Focus on the verse you wrote out above. Just like a newborn baby craves his mother's milk, so you must crave the "pure milk" of the Word. Oh boy. We need to stop for a moment and let that one sink in. Are you craving the *pure milk* of Scripture? Or are you content with a spiritual pacifier?

Have you ever watched a mama bird feed her young? As mama arrives, the babies open their mouths expectantly. Mama then places her beak inside baby's open mouth and proceeds to feed her little one regurgitated worm. Gross! Have you ever stopped to consider why she does that? As a baby, it is incapable of finding its own food, let alone able to properly handle the solid food yet.

Too many of us are spiritually undernourished. Why? Because we are sucking on spiritual pacifiers instead of feeding on the real thing. We are content to sit in church on Sunday and listen to the preacher feed us from the Bible—regurgitating the spiritual food he's already chewed upon and eaten—instead of digging into Scripture for ourselves. We think it's okay to read Biblical principles out of a devotional book without ever opening the Bible to discover God's truth for ourselves.

Now, don't misunderstand me. Going to church, learning from the teaching of others, reading great devotional books, are all good things to do. But if you are dependent upon those things to feed you spiritually, you're sucking on a pacifier. You're allowing someone else to chew up the food for you. They are spitting it out and you're gobbling it up. That's not enough. That alone will not give you the spiritual nourishment you need to grow.

The Feeding Schedule

One thing I've learned in raising four children, and in watching my kids raise our grandchildren, is that babies don't drink all the milk they can in an hour on Sunday—then go the rest of the week without eating. They have a feeding schedule. They eat every few hours. Why? Because they can hold on to just so much food at any given time. As their body consumes and digests, it also burns up energy. Eventually they need more nutrients to keep going.

What's your spiritual "feeding schedule"? We need to consume God's Word daily. Do you really think that you can stuff yourself on Sunday's regurgitated meal and live your Christian life off of that one feeding for the rest of the week? Of course not! Yet that's exactly what many of us try to do spiritually.

On Sunday, we gobble up the food that someone else has eaten and spit out, and maybe—just maybe—a few times during the week we'll open a devotional and snack on something that someone has fed upon and then spoon-fed back to us. Then, when temptation hits, when trials come our way, when the stress of life begins to drag us down, we wonder why we aren't able to handle it. We can't understand why we're so weak and unable to stand up against the attack.

❏ Why don't we feed on God's Word more than we do?

Christians who aren't daily consuming God's Word are trying to satisfy their hunger with pacifiers. As a result, they are severely malnourished. It's not enough to sit under a Bible teacher for an hour a week—no matter how great that preacher may be. The meal he's serving up behind the pulpit should be just the appetizer. The main course should be consumed all week long. We need to be in the Word daily for ourselves!

> "I have not departed from the commands of (God's) lips; I have treasured the words of His mouth more than my daily bread." (Job 23:12, addition mine)

LOOK AT YOUR BIBLE

The pressing question we have to address here is this: How do I get to that point? What must I do in order to experience true delight in God's Word? How does a person learn to actually treasure God's Word more than anything else?

It begins with a personal relationship with Jesus Christ. The unsaved don't care for the God of the Word, so it only makes sense that they won't care for the Word of God. They don't see the need for it. They don't understand it, simply because they can't.[4] Until they have a personal relationship with Christ, they never will.

> **Key Thought:** *Do you know Jesus Christ as your personal Lord and Savior? This is the first step toward delighting in God's Word.*

Second, before we can truly delight in God's Word we must understand that the Bible is not just another book.
- It's not some sci-fi story you pull off the shelf and read all the way through in a weekend—although it does tell accounts of out-of-this-world experiences.
- It's not a storybook that you read just before bedtime—although it does tell the story of God's redemption of mankind.
- It's not a romance novel that you read while curled up by the fire on a cold winter's day—although it does share how God demonstrated His amazing love for man by sacrificing Himself on our behalf.
- It's not a history textbook that you teach to a class of bored students—although it does tell the history of mankind from creation to his eternal destination.
- It's not a how-to book for do-it-yourselfers that you read when you want to fix something—although it does show us how to repair our broken relationship with God and how to live a life that brings glory to our Heavenly Father.

The Bible is God's inspired word written to you and me to show us who God is and who we are before Him. It shows our need for a

Savior, and how God provided for that need through the person of Jesus Christ.

In the Bible, you discover God's desire to have a personal relationship with you—and within its pages He shows you exactly how you can know Him, not just as your Creator and Judge, but as your Savior, Father, and eternal Friend.

The Bible teaches you how to live a life that is holy and pure. It shows you how to say no to sin and yield your life in full and complete surrender to God—living a life that in every way glorifies Him. What an amazing book!

The Bible is God speaking directly to you—to help you cope with every issue in life you will ever face. As you listen to the Holy Spirit and choose to yield to His leadership in your life, He helps you face your temptations, handle all of life's trials, and teaches you how to find peace, happiness, and contentment through an intimate relationship with your Heavenly Father.

The Bible is the instrument God uses to provide you with power and strength, knowledge, understanding, wisdom, and hope. Within its pages you will find life and food for your soul. Can you begin to understand why you need to delight in God's Word?

- Do you want to live a life that glorifies God? Live according to the Word of God.[5]
- Do you want to live a sin-free life? Hide God's Word in your heart.[6]
- Do you need to find strength and encouragement during times of stress, suffering, and sorrow? Read your Bible and let it uplift you.[7]
- Do you feel lost and need a sense of direction? Open the Scriptures and let God guide you.[8]
- Are you looking for hope? You'll find it within the pages of your Bible.[9]

When you begin to see God's Word in this light, you can say with the Psalmist, "Oh, how I love your law! I meditate on it all day long."[10]

CHRISTIAN COWS
❏ Write out Psalm 1:2.

Note in the verse above that the one who is "blessed" is the one who delights so much in God's Word that he *meditates* on it day and night. Not only does that person long to read God's Word, he thinks about what he read all day long. He is seriously contemplating what God has said to him and how he can apply it to his life.

When you are truly delighting in God's Word, you are going to do more than just read it—you're going to meditate on it. You are going to ask God to show you how to apply its truths and principles to your daily living.

By the way, the word "meditate" in Psalm 1:2 is written in the imperfect tense. It's what I call a perfectly imperfect word. You see, the meditation David is talking about is an action that is not yet completed—it's imperfect. It is something that must be repeated over and over again. Listening to God's Word isn't enough. Reading it doesn't suffice. You just can't get enough of what God has to say. You find yourself thinking about it throughout your day.
- Did you read your Bible today?
- Do you remember what you read?
- Have you been thinking about how it applies to you?
- Have you been asking God to show you how to live it out in everything you think, say, and do today?

That is meditating on God's Word. Meditation is not some mystical, Eastern religion-based activity. It's not about sitting cross-legged on the floor with eyes closed, fingertips barely touching while you quietly hum.

In Scripture, the verb "meditate" refers to breaking something down into small, chewable pieces. Meditating makes it easier to digest what you've eaten so that you can draw strength and nourishment from it, similar to a cow chewing her cud.

Did you know that before a cow can chew its cud, she first has to eat some grass? If there's no grass in her stomach, there will be no cud to chew later on. In a similar way, it's impossible for you to meditate on God's Word if you are not first feeding upon it. You must read, study, and even memorize the Word before you can ever begin to meditate upon it.

Now, I'm not a cowboy. In fact, I know little about cows other than they eat grass, say moo, and give milk. So, I had to do some research. Here's what I've learned: after sufficiently chewing the grass, 'Ol Bessie swallows it, sending it into the first of four chambers in her stomach. A little while later, she regurgitates that chewed-up grass and begins chewing it again. As she chews, she is breaking down the grass further. She then swallows it again, sending it into the second chamber of her stomach. Later she will bring it up again and chew on it some more. Each time she chews on it, she is breaking it down more to enable proper digestion.

That is a great example of meditation. Every time you open your Bible and read it, every time you dig into and study it, every time you commit a verse to memory, you are feeding upon the Word of God. You are chewing on it and then swallowing it, taking it into storage for later use.

Then, periodically throughout the day, you bring it back to mind and think about it; evaluating, scrutinizing, seeking to know and understand just what God is saying, and how it applies to you. You then "swallow" it down again, storing it for later.

You keep your heart open to the leading of the Holy Spirit throughout the day. You're asking Him to guide you into a deeper understanding of what you've learned. As the day goes on, you again bring it up and chew on it some more—thinking about the principle God is teaching you and how you can apply it to your life. Here's the cool thing—God will give you practical opportunities throughout the day to apply what you've learned. For example, you've read some Scripture during breakfast—you fed upon God's Word. As you progress through the morning you begin to think about what you read. You think about what it means, about how it applies to your life, and how you should adjust your choices and actions accordingly.

During your lunch break, you sit there eating your leftover ham between two dry slices of bread while thinking more about that text of Scripture you read this morning. You are definitely seeing that God is showing you an area of your life that needs attention. You utter a quick prayer, asking your Father to reveal to you what He wants you to do, and to give you the strength to apply it to your life.

That evening someone makes a comment that upsets you. Immediately that verse of Scripture you've been meditating on all day pops into your mind. Smiling, you reply with a Biblical, loving response instead of the sharp retort you would have given yesterday. That is the process of meditation.

MY MOST FAVORITE FOOD IS...
If you are going to grow spiritually, you must feed daily on God's word and meditate on it.
> "Oh, how I love your law! I meditate on it all day long." (Psalm 119:97)

David shouted from the top of his lungs, "I love feeding upon God's Word!" He loved it! He enjoyed it so much that he had a deep craving for it. He wasn't happy—he wasn't satisfied—until he was able to sit down and consume it. Then, throughout the day he kept thinking about what God had spoken to him. He clung to every word he read—it was his life-blood.

Do you feel that way about God's Word? Do you enjoy being in the word so much that you have a deep craving for it?

GIVE IT SOME THOUGHT
- ❏ Every time you open your Bible, what are you *doing* with what God reveals to you?

- ❏ Are you *considering* God's Word during the day? When you encounter an unplanned-for situation, what are your first thoughts? When a boss is demanding, or a client is frustrating you; when the children aren't obeying, or the car breaks down in the middle of rush hour, what goes racing through your mind?

Endnotes
1. Psalm 1:2 (NIV '84)
2. Ezekiel 3:1-3
3. Psalm 119:92
4. 1 Corinthians 2:14
5. Psalm 119:9
6. Psalm 119:11
7. Psalm 119:28, 50
8. Psalm 119:105
9. Psalm 119:114, 147
10. Psalm 119:97 (NIV '84)

> "If you hold to my teaching, you are really my
> disciples. Then you will know the truth,
> and the truth will set you free."
> John 8:31-32

NINE: DECEIVED, DUPED, AND DOUBLE-CROSSED

In Chapter One we talked about the evil tactics Satan uses as he engages you in guerilla warfare. We also pointed out that taking you down is not his endgame. That's not his goal. You're not a threat to his plan for world-domination. God is.

Satan knows you, as a born-again believer, are God's precious child. That is exactly why he's unloading his arsenal upon you. Satan hates God. Satan wants to hurt God. Satan knows that God loves you more than anything. His surest way to hurt God is to attack the love of God's heart—you.

Satan's primary strategy in his war against God is to attack your mind. He knows that if he can impress your thinking, he can impact your living. That's so powerful I am compelled to repeat it. Satan knows that when he impresses your thinking he will impact your living!
- ❏ Write out Isaiah 26:3.

What a glorious promise! When your mind is totally focused on God, you are in a place of complete safety. In that place you're able to experience the quiet contentment and soundness of mind that is peace. You can have complete confidence in God, no matter what may be happening around you, all because your mind is fixed on your Heavenly Father!

Who doesn't want to have peace?
- Want peace in your marriage? Focus on God.
- Want peace in your finances? Focus on God.
- Want peace in the midst of your trials and testing? Focus on God!

When your mind is "steadfast"—leaning entirely upon God for everything you need—God promises to keep you in the place of peace. And not just any peace—perfect peace.

Does that mean that you won't have any conflict, trouble, or trials? No. Paul describes this peace as a "peace of God, which surpasses all understanding." It's a peace that "will guard your hearts and minds in Christ Jesus."[1] No matter what may be happening around you, no matter what the situation, the conflict, the trial, or test—no matter what—when your mind is fixed on the Father, His peace will guard your heart and mind. You will not be sucked under by the powerful pull of the enemy.

When you fully trust in the Lord, when your confidence is placed in the Savior of your soul, you "will be like a tree planted by the water that sends out its roots by the stream. It does not fear when heat comes; its leaves are always green. It has no worries in a year of drought and never fails to bear fruit."[2]

Did you catch that? The heat of temptation *will* come. You *will* experience the trials of drought. But when your trust and confidence is firmly placed on God, you will bear fruit!

SATAN'S MODUS OPERANDI
Criminologists have learned that, whatever their specialty—burglary, theft, arson, etc.—professional criminals have an M.O. (modus operandi—Latin for "operating method"). Each criminal

has a particular way of operating and will tend to adhere to that way whenever perpetrating the crime.

Did you know Satan has an M.O. as well? Paul says of Satan, "We are not unaware of his schemes."[3] In other words, we already know his operating method. That means you don't have to go into battle against your spiritual foe ignorant of the tactics he's going to use against you.

> **Key Thought:** *Satan attacks your mind with lies to turn you against God's will.*

❑ We never have to guess at what God wants from and for us. Where must you go to discover God's will?

❑ Write out James 1:22.

Here's my point: God's will is revealed in God's Word. James warns us that when you choose to just listen to God's Word and do nothing about it, you are being deceived. That is exactly what Satan wants—he wants you to be deceived. In fact, he is a master at deception. Jesus said that Satan does "not (hold) to the truth, for there is no truth in him. When he lies, he speaks his native language, for he is a liar and the father of lies."[4] Revelation 12:9 tells us that Satan is "that ancient serpent...who leads the whole world astray." The Devil is a master deceiver.

"DECEVED"

> "Now the serpent was more crafty than any other beast of the field that the LORD God had made. He said to the woman, 'Did God actually say, 'You shall not eat of any tree in the garden'?' And the woman

said to the serpent, 'We may eat of the fruit of the trees in the garden, but God said, 'You shall not eat of the fruit of the tree that is in the midst of the garden, neither shall you touch it, lest you die.' But the serpent said to the woman, 'You will not surely die. For God knows that when you eat of it your eyes will be opened, and you will be like God, knowing good and evil.' So when the woman saw that the tree was good for food, and that it was a delight to the eyes, and that the tree was to be desired to make one wise, she took of its fruit and ate, and she also gave some to her husband who was with her, and he ate. Then the eyes of both were opened, and they knew that they were naked. And they sewed fig leaves together and made themselves loincloths." (Genesis 3:1-7)

Satan wanted to attack God. He chose to do so by attacking the one part of God's creation that meant the most to Him. Interestingly, Satan didn't go for a direct, frontal assault. Nor did he use some form of excruciating torture. He simply started an outwardly innocent conversation focused around one simple goal: to change the way Eve thought about God.

Remember, if he can impress your thinking, he will impact your living.
- ❏ Write out 1 Corinthians 11:3.

- ❏ What was Paul afraid of?

Here is a critical point: Satan attacked Eve's *mind*. Paul knew that Satan would use the same M.O. on us as well. Why? Because "as a man thinketh in his heart, so is he."[5] What you think will eventually become what you do. When your thoughts are focused on King Me, your choices and actions will be for King Me. That's why we are commanded to take captive all our thoughts,[6] and think only on godly things.[7]

> Key Thought: *Satan's target is your mind. His weapon is lies. His purpose—to persuade you to live for King Me instead of God.*

Satan wants to draw you away from the Almighty God of the Universe. He hates God, and he is going to try to use you to wound Him.

In his assault on Eve's mind, Satan used three subtle steps to deceive her into buying his lie.

STEP #1: QUESTION GOD'S WORD
He began with a seemingly innocent question.
- ❏ Write out Genesis 3:1.

Did you notice what Satan did here? All he did was pose a simple question. "Did God really say that? What if you heard wrong? What if you're misinterpreting what He meant? In fact, what did He mean?" In short, by asking Eve that seemingly innocent question, he began to cast the tiniest shadow of doubt in her mind. This doubt would eventually grow into a life-changing action.

Satan didn't attack God's Word directly. He didn't actually deny that God had spoken. He didn't try to force Eve to believe that God never actually said anything of importance. He simply posed a question.

TOMATO, TOMAHTOE — POTATO, POTAHTOE
Notice Eve's response to Satan's question. "The woman said to the serpent, 'We may eat fruit from the trees in the garden'" (Genesis

3:2). Seems like an innocent enough response, right? In fact, she spoke the truth—more or less. She was indeed able to eat from the trees in the garden. However, look carefully at what she said to Satan. Can you see any indication that the seed of doubt has already begun to grow in Eve's mind?

Do you recall what God actually said? "You are free to eat from any tree in the garden" (Genesis 2:16). Do you see what Eve did? She stepped directly into Satan's trap—she chose to take away from God's word. She left out one very important word. "One word?" you ask. "Why kick up a fuss over one word?"

What is that one word she omitted? Eve neglected to tell Satan that she was "free" to eat from any tree in the garden. Why is that so significant?

❏ Write out Matthew 5:18.

Luke recorded it this way, "It is easier for heaven and earth to disappear than for the least stroke of a pen to drop out of the Law" (Luke 16:17, NIV '84). There are a couple of things here worth noting. First, Jesus refers to "the smallest letter" and "the least stroke of a pen." The King James Version of the Bible uses the words "jot and tittle."

The "jot" is actually the smallest letter of the Hebrew alphabet. It's called the *"yodh."* That letter occupies proportionately about the same amount of space as that of the English apostrophe. Although the "yodh" is the smallest Hebrew letter, it carries just as much power and significance as any other letter of the alphabet.

Consider this: letters spell words; words compose sentences; sentences reveal God's truth. How you spell a word is important. The spelling of a word determines the meaning and purpose of that word.

Take the word "car," for instance. When you see that word, you know it has a specific meaning. However, if you spell that word a different way, changing out only one letter, you have a totally different word. For example, remove the "r" and replace it with a "t" and, voilà, you have an entirely different word that has an entirely different meaning. The car has now become a cat.

Single letters change words and thus they also change the meaning of the word. Jesus' promise in Matthew 5:18 is that not one "yodh," not one single letter of Scripture (no matter how small or insignificant it might seem) would fail. Every letter is equally inspired as is every word. God says what He means, and He means what He says—every letter of it.

Looking once again at Matthew 5:18, we see that Jesus also talks about the "least stroke of a pen" (called the "tittle"). The tittle is even smaller than the "yodh." Whereas the yodh is a whole letter, a tittle is only part of a letter. When the tittle is present, it forms a specific letter. When the tittle is absent, then it's a totally different letter.

Confused? Let me see if I can help.
- ❑ In the space below, write in large letters the word "Fun" (with a capital "F").

- ❑ Now, I want you to add a "tittle" to that word. Put the right side of a half circle (like the right side of a parenthesis) on the right of the letter "F", creating a new word…"Pun."
  By adding the "tittle" you changed the letter. By changing the letter, you changed the meaning of the word. That little tittle made a big change.

- ❑ Finally, I want you to add one more "tittle" to this new word. Put a backward hash "\" underneath the circle part of the letter "P", creating another new word…"Run."

> Once again, by adding another "tittle" you changed the letter. By changing the letter, you changed the meaning of the word. Oh, the power of the tittle!

So, not only are the words of the Bible important to God; even the dotting of the "i's" and the crossing of the "t's" were inspired by God.[8] God views his Word very seriously, and so should we.

Now, let's go back to our initial question: What is so significant about Eve's omission of the word "free"? When she omitted the word "free," Eve painted a picture of a selfish, unloving, and stingy God, withholding the best from His creation. Oh, my friend, never take away from God's Word. When we begin to change what God says, it becomes much easier to disobey what God says.

> **Key Thought:** *Every word of God is important to God, and should be to us as well.*

In Psalm 119, verses 11 and 105, David declares that God's Word keeps us from sinning because it is a lamp showing us where to go and how to live. Hebrews 4:12 and 2 Timothy 3:16-17 are clear that God's word is living, powerful, and productive when you read it, meditate on it, and obey it.

Yes, Satan planted a tiny seed of doubt in Eve's mind—but she chose to think about it, to dwell on it. She allowed her mind to play with that seed, and as a result, her response to the Devil was tainted. Even today we must be very careful not to take away from God's Word. Satan wants to deceive your mind and draw you away from the simplicity that is in Christ. Just as he did with Eve, he will begin by getting you to question God's Word. "Did God really say that?"

When we begin to doubt God, we aren't so quick to turn to Him for the answers to our questions—or doubts. It becomes easier to detach ourselves from God's Word, leading us to the next step—denying the truth of what God actually said.

STEP #2: DENY GOD'S WORD

❑ Write out Genesis 3:4-5.

After Eve responded to Satan's first step, he knew he had her right where he wanted her. Conspiratorially he grinned, leaned forward a bit, and whispered into her ear, "C'mon, Eve. Do you really think that you're going to die? You're not going to die; God's making that up. He's lying to you because He's afraid you'll become just like Him—and that threatens Him."

> **Key Thought:** *When Satan convinces you to* doubt *God's Truth, you're one small step away from* denying *God's Truth.*

Once the seed of doubt had taken root in Eve's mind, her uncontrolled thoughts took over, drawing her ever further away from God's truth. The result: she saw nothing wrong with questioning God. That opened her up to thinking it was okay to add her own spin to His sacred word.

Consider what God had said. "You must not eat from the tree of the knowledge of good and evil, for when you eat of it you will surely die" (Genesis 2:17, NIV '84). Can you see what Eve did? First, she omitted a word. God had said "you will surely die." What did Eve neglect to say? She left out the word "surely," a word God used to speak of the surety, the fact, the absolute truth of what would happen if they chose to disobey.

Second, she added to God's Word. Eve told Satan that God instructed them to not even touch the fruit. But isn't that a good thing? After all, everyone is better off if you just avoid the fruit completely. It makes sense.

When Eve added to what God had said, she did two very serious things.

1. She turned God into something that He is not. She painted the picture of a God who is stern and rigid, less kind and generous. The fact is, God had lovingly given them an entire garden with more food than they could ever eat. Satan successfully steered her thinking away from that fact and got her to focus on the one thing God said she couldn't have. What kind of loving, caring, selfless God is that?

2. By adding the words "you must not touch it," she changed God's command into a burden too heavy to bear. She was already doubting and questioning God's Word. She had already created a false image of God, making Him into something He is not. Now, to make matters worse, she saw God as denying her the one thing she wanted most in this world—to be like God! The load God was expecting her to bear became too much.

> **Key Thought:** *God will never give you more than you can bear—never.*[9]

STEP #3: REPLACE TRUTH WITH A LIE

Satan is waging an all-out war against your mind with his lies, to keep you from growing in your walk with God. Once he has you questioning the truth of God's Word, you begin to listen to his denial of God's Word. Then he moves in for the final blow.

> **Key Thought:** *Satan inserts his own lies in place of God's Word, convincing you the lie is truth.*

"God knows that if you eat the fruit of this tree, you will know the truth. You will see just what kind of God He really is. You will finally see how He's been using you. He doesn't care about you.

Read Genesis 3:4-5. Can you identify the lie? Adam and Eve were already created after the image of God,[11] but Satan got them to question and then doubt that truth. Once they did that, it was easy for them to accept his lie substituted as truth.

Sound familiar? Isn't that exactly how Satan works today? His M.O. hasn't changed. Satan's lie, "You will be like God," still motivates and controls mankind today. Every time you put King Me on the throne of your heart, you are buying into the enemy's lie that you can control your life and determine your own destiny. I want, I need … I deserve!

The truth permeating Scripture is that no one can be like God.[12] Satan is a liar. And yet so many of us are buying into the lie, trying to do life on our own, in our own power and wisdom—turning to God only when our own efforts have failed us.

When we try to figure out life without looking to God's Word for direction, when we attempt to make choices without seeking the guidance of our Heavenly Father, we become vulnerable to input from ungodly influences. Those influences will *never* lead us down the right path. They will try to sway us away from God.

When we begin to doubt God's Word and deny God's truth, allowing Satan's deceitful lies to take the place of God's absolute truth, we will no longer see the necessity for God's Word. The result: we will begin to live a life apart from God's will.

By using the strategy he did, Satan persuaded Eve to consider the tree separately from what God had said. He influenced her thinking with his lies so that she doubted and questioned God's Word. That's when she was open to rejecting God's truth. The final blow came when she accepted Satan's lies as the truth and reached out, not only taking the fruit but eating it as well.

THINK — JUST THINK
When you doubt the Word of God, you begin to also doubt the God of the Word. As a result, you begin to trust only in King Me. Thoughts of honoring God are now crowded out by thoughts of all the perceived "rights" that are being denied you. You begin to see God's standards as a harsh and cruel burden you have to carry. This in turn causes you to see God as unloving and uncaring.

From there, it's much easier to allow your mind to linger on the pleasures that sin affords, and you begin to think about life apart from the absolute truth of God's Word. Finally, it is a very short step toward outright disobedience to your Heavenly Father.

> **Key Thought:** *All Satan has to do is convince you to choose to think about life apart from the Word and will of God—you'll do the rest.*

Oh, my friend, we must understand how vital it is that we consider all of life in light of God's Word. God's truth must always be our guide in every aspect of life.

That's why I strongly urge you to be in the Scriptures DAILY! It is fundamentally imperative that you continuously saturate your mind with God's truth. You see, "no lie comes from the truth."[13] Daily you face the same choice that Eve did—God's truth or Satan's lie? When you dilute and change God's truth, it is easy for you to reject that truth, believe the lie, and choose to sin.

Contrary to what he wants you to believe, Satan is not your friend. He doesn't care about your pleasure, enjoyment, or happiness. He wants to hurt God, and he will use you to do it if he can.

❑ Write out 1 Peter 5:8-9.

Peter says we are to be "self-controlled" (sober-minded). You need to always be in your right mind, thinking correctly. Why? Because the Devil is on the hunt, looking for someone to devour.

When a lioness is on the hunt, she knows that the best target is the weak one. When she comes upon a herd of antelope, she crouches low in the grass and patiently waits. She's watching to see which one is the weakest. This is what Satan does.

He's looking for the Christian who is weak in the faith, the one who isn't hiding God's Word in his heart, focusing his thoughts on glorifying God. You should always be in your right mind, thinking properly—on guard against the attack of the enemy.[14]

GIVE IT SOME THOUGHT

❑ Why does Satan attack your mind with his lies?

❑ How are you going to counter his attacks?

❑ How can you know whether it's the enemy speaking his lies to you, or the Holy Spirit revealing God's truth?

Endnotes
1. Philippians 4:7
2. Jeremiah 17:7-8 (NIV '84)
3. 2 Corinthians 2:11 (NIV '84)
4. John 8:43-44 (NIV '84)
5. Proverbs 23:7 (KJV)
6. 2 Corinthians 10:5
7. Philippians 4:8
8. 2 Timothy 3:16-17
9. 1 John 5:3-4
10. Deuteronomy 4:2; 12:32; Proverbs 30:6
11. Genesis 1:26-27
12. See Exodus 8:10; 9:14; 2 Samuel 7:22; 1 Chronicles 17:20; Isaiah 46:9.
13. 1 John 2:21
14. Proverbs 4:23

> "When tempted, no one should say, 'God is tempting me.' For God cannot be tempted by evil, nor does He tempt anyone."
> James 1:13

TEN: CONSIDER THE SOURCE

Everyone struggles at some level with daily temptation; you can't avoid it. We tend to blame other people or other things for our choice to sin. In fact, we even blame God. After all, we reason, He let this temptation happen!
- ❏ Write out James 1:13-15.

Notice in verse 14 James says each of us "is tempted when he is lured (dragged away) and enticed by his own desire." Think with me about the words "dragged away."
- ❏ When you think of someone being dragged away, what comes to mind?

Being "dragged away" almost gives the idea that you're being kidnapped—taken kicking and screaming, against your will. But that is *not* what this phrase means here. James is not referring to something that takes you unawares and against your will.

NO FISHING ZONE

James is using a fishing term that is literally translated "drawn away." He is referring to being lured away from a place of safety—much like a fish is lured.

The purpose of a lure is to disguise the deadly hook. Think about it. If I toss a hook in the water without any kind of lure attached to it, how successful will I be in catching a fish? Not at all. However, by providing an enticement (lure) to the fish, the entire scenario changes. The probability of landing that trophy fish greatly increases.

Different lures catch different fish. What is the lure that draws you away from *your* walk with Christ? The answer is found in James 1:14. We are lured and drawn away by "our own evil desires." That is, there is a particular lust or a craving you have for sinful pleasure and you allow yourself to *think about* how to satisfy it.

As you allow that craving to rattle around in your mind, you begin to play with the idea of giving in. You begin to seek out reasons why it would be okay "just this time." The more you think about it, the more appealing it becomes. The more you justify sinful behavior, the sooner you finally give in to the temptation and choose to sin.

- ❏ What is it you like so much, or want so badly, that you choose to sin to get it or keep it? Be honest.

- ❏ Why do we flirt around with sin? Why do we even allow our minds to think about it, letting it divert our hearts away from God?

- ❏ What are the potential consequences to giving in?

❏ If we choose not to give in, what are the losses?

❏ If we choose not to give in, what are the gains?

In verse 14 James says your sin "entices" you. It appeals to your sinful, fleshly desires for ease and pleasure, and it brings a type of excitement and arousal, even a sense of comfort.

Here's how it works: first you begin to think about it. Thinking about it feels good. Thinking about it increases the anticipation and the desire for fleshly comfort and pleasure. Then you let your mind dwell on it—it's not just a thought; it has become an experience, a fantasy. You play around with the possibilities. You entertain those thoughts, letting them build in your mind. Eventually you choose to act upon those thoughts.

> **Key Thought:** *When you entertain wrong thoughts, those thoughts will eventually produce wrong actions.*

For example, if you allow your mind to dwell on improper sexual thoughts you will eventually act upon those thoughts. You might go to the Internet and visit adult-oriented websites. You might look upon someone in an improper way. You may develop unrealistic expectations in your marriage. You may seek out an extra-marital relationship. You might even commit a crime, all in the name of sexual lust.

When you entertain prideful thoughts, your actions will be self-focused and self-purposed—geared to draw attention to "King Me" for the sole purpose of pleasing only self—usually at the expense of others. When you entertain thoughts of fear, anger, anxiety, bitterness (and the list goes on), your actions will fall into step accordingly. When you intentionally focus your thoughts on glorifying God, what will happen? You will give God the glory in all that you say and do!

James is telling us that we sin because we see the lure of a sinful pleasure, it entices us, we think about it, we play around with the idea of it and, if not properly dealt with, the result is that we commit a sinful act, which in turn leads to separation from God.

HARD ~~HAT~~ HEART AREA
One of Satan's major battle tactics is that of keeping Christians thinking they are defeated, still in bondage to sin. When he accomplishes this, he has succeeded in diminishing our potential for the kingdom of God. If he can induce you to feel defeated in your sin, to believe that you're never going to change—after all, you're only human and you still have that sinful nature—then you will eventually give up trying. You will learn to accept that sinful aspect of your life and eventually even embrace it. You develop a hard heart.

❏ What is a "hard heart," and how does a person develop one?

❏ What are the dangers of having a hard heart?

Any time you choose to not deal with a sin issue in your life, it will ultimately lead to a hardened heart. A hard heart happens when you hear God's truth, believe what He says is indeed truth, yet repeatedly choose to do nothing about it.

Every time you decide to ignore God's Word, your heart hardens ever so slightly. The temptation becomes stronger and you fight it less. Sin has a stronger hold in your life and the conviction you feel over that sin loses some of its grip.

Every time you recognize a sin in your life, feel the convicting power of the Holy Spirit, and yet do nothing about it, you become less sensitive—your conscience is being "seared as with a hot iron."[1] Over time, you become callous to the promptings of the Holy Spirit and suppress His fire;[2] just like when you close the door on a lantern, though the light is still there, it no longer shines for others to see.

I want to encourage you that there is hope! Paul writes in Philippians 1:6 that he is "confident of this, that He who began a good work in you *will* carry it on to completion until the day of Christ." You see, "It is God who works in you to will and to work for *His good purpose.*"[3] God has a plan for your life.[4] He is not going to allow sin to thwart His purpose. He will never leave you to the wolves.

Don't allow yourself to become bogged down in trying to figure out *how* to have victory over sin in your life. Focus your attention on growing in your relationship with God, who is able to strengthen you to do all things,[5] and victory will follow!

Do The Math

The sin you give in to is not the only sin you will struggle with. Do the math.

- $1 + 1 + 1 = ?$

Don't tell my elementary school math teacher, but the correct answer to the above equation is "more than one" or "too many." One sin inevitably leads to another, and then to another. Once you become comfortable with a particular sin in your life, it is only a matter of time until other issues arise.

For example, the husband who has been secretly looking at pornography isn't only dealing with the sin of lust. By keeping it secret, he is guilty of deceit and lying as well. If the sin continues to grow, his battle with such sins as pride, anger, and bitterness will deepen.

> **Key Thought:** *Sin will always result in death.*[6]

Whenever you sin, there is *always* a death that follows. Again, let's use the husband entrenched in pornography as an example. He is battling with sin on a number of different fronts (lust, pride, anger, controlling fear, etc.). As a result, his sin has brought death to his relationship with his wife.

The marriage relationship begins to deteriorate. He becomes withdrawn, self-focused, and self-obsessed. He no longer reaches out to her, caring for her, and loving her the way he used to. Their physical relationship also begins to die. This in turn causes *her* to withdraw, eventually destroying her love for him—another death. Sin will always result in some kind of death; something is always destroyed.

Too often we listen to the lies of the enemy: "I'm just human; nobody is perfect. I am always going to struggle with sin anyway, so why fight it?" Listen carefully: all believers, including you, have the ability to say no to temptation.

So, don't you ever, *ever* let the lie of the enemy convince you that you cannot have victory in the face of temptation, especially over the temptations that so easily entangle you,[7] because God says otherwise. God is truth and no lie ever comes from the truth.[8]

BUT I'M SUCH A UNIQUE PERSON!
There is no, "But, Steve, you don't understand." There is no, "But my situation is different." Look at 1 Corinthians 10:13 again: "*No temptation has seized you except what is common to man ...*" Think about that. Paul uses the word "no," which is an absolute negative. Absolutely not a single temptation will ever come upon you that is totally unique to you. Not one.

We all struggle with temptation. Every Christian battles every day with sin issues. Paul said it is *common* to man. We all experience the same temptations. It may have a different face and be experienced in a different way, but at the core it's still the same temptation.

It's a war, my friend.[9] You will always be tempted; it's part of the Christian life. But you never have to give in to the temptation. You never *have* to sin. Others have experienced the same temptation and have been victorious over it—so can you!

❏ How do you typically respond to temptation?

❏ Why do you choose to respond that way?

❏ When does temptation become sin?

God understands the intimidating pull of temptation. You feel like it is going to overwhelm you, sweeping you away in its powerful flow. Paul says that <u>no</u> temptation has *seized* you (or taken you).

> **Key Thought:** *God's promise to every Christian is that no temptation, even though it feels like it has dug its nasty claws deep into you, will be so strong that you cannot stand with Christ in the face of it.*

Again, let me remind you that Paul said, "no temptation." Not a single one ever has been, nor ever will be, stronger than God. Got it? Good!

I love it when I see the words "but God" in Scripture.[10] No temptation, even the one that gives you the feeling of powerlessness, is stronger than God. "*But God* is faithful," my friend. That word "faithful" refers to one who has been repeatedly proven trustworthy in the execution of his promise and the discharge of his official duty.

The one who is faithful can be fully and completely relied upon to keep his word and do exactly what he has promised. So here is a question for you: Who is faithful, fully trustworthy, and completely reliable to keep his every word and promise? Who will, with the temptation, help you to endure? The answer is: God, the Almighty, Holy, all-powerful, sovereign Creator of the universe!

❑ How does God show His faithfulness in the midst of your temptation?

God is faithful. He knows about your temptation and He has promised that He will give you the ability to endure. He doesn't want you to be defeated or discouraged. He doesn't want you to feel the only choice is to sin.

God will not let you be tempted beyond what you can bear. This does not mean that you will never experience a temptation. Nor does it mean that the temptations you do experience won't seem overwhelming at times. It does, however, mean that God is in control, even when you are being tempted. In the midst of that temptation, you can fully trust that He will not permit that temptation to be more than you can deal with.

❑ Why does God allow temptation to enter your life?

Let me be quick to remind you that God is not the one who tempts you to sin.[11] If Satan had his way, that temptation would bring about your destruction. But God uses it as a way to show you that there is an area of weakness in your life that needs to be dealt with, so that you can have a more intimate relationship with Him.

Through that temptation, God is providing you with an opportunity to discover what sin issues you are still struggling with, and where King Me is still sitting on the throne. In the midst of that temptation, He shows you how to escape—how to stand firm in truth and not give in.

> "No temptation has seized you except what is common to man. And God is faithful; he will not let you be tempted beyond what you can bear. But when you are tempted, he will also provide a way out so that you can stand up under it." (1 Corinthians 10:13 NIV '84)

Paul uses the words "can bear" in the present tense, active voice, and indicative mood. Let me explain.

- *Present tense* refers to the immediate here and now, in real time. The action being described (in this case, enduring the temptation) is happening right now...right now...right now. Always in the present, always able to endure.
- *Active voice* means you are the one doing the action—in this case, *you* are enduring the temptation. I can't do it for you. You can't do it for me.
- *Indicative mood* means it is a simple statement of fact. In other words, it is a plain truth that as you personally, right this very moment, are going through a temptation, no matter how overwhelming it may seem, you have the resources and ability to endure it. God makes sure of that. You *can* endure —you don't have to sin!

The key is *how* you deal with your temptation when it comes. Note that the temptation will come. Paul says, "*when* you are tempted," not "*if* you are tempted."

James tells us to "consider it pure joy ... whenever you face trials of many kinds."[12] We will always struggle with temptation. The key is how you manage it. How you handle it begins with your mind— what you allow yourself to think about in the midst of the temptation.

- Write out Colossians 3:2.

- When are you to do what Colossians 3:2 commands you to do?

- How well are you doing with that?

If you look at the temptation with a defeatist attitude, you will end up being defeated. However, if you see the temptation as God revealing something in your life that needs to be dealt with so that you can mature and conform to the image of Christ, then you will take a totally different approach to the temptation. This is the way you are able to endure it.

- When you intentionally view your temptation as an opportunity to grow in your walk with God, what will be different about how you respond to that temptation?

"God is faithful, and he will not let you be tempted beyond your ability, but with the temptation he will also provide the way of escape, that you may be able to endure it."[13] The way out that God provides is not that you will no longer experience the temptation. That "way out" would not help you grow closer to him. That "way out" would not help you become more like Christ.

That kind of "way out" gives you the opportunity to slip back into your contented way of living. It makes it easy for you, and God isn't about making life easy. Rather, as you are *going through* the temptation, you are to focus your mind on the things of God; focus your attention on what it is that God is revealing to you and what you need to do to deal with it. As you do, you will receive exactly what you need to be able to "endure" the temptation—standing up under the pressure, not being crushed by it.

Go to God's Word. Dig into Scripture. Study it. Memorize it. Meditate on it. Then, as God shows you truth from His Word, as He reveals to you the path to victory, apply it to your life—choosing daily to live by it.

❏   Write out Galatians 5:16.

Live (walk) by the Spirit. This is your way of escape. God isn't saying that you will no longer face this temptation, but that it will no longer feel overbearing and overpowering. You will be able to endure (bear up under) the temptation patiently, because now you know how to handle it victoriously; it can no longer crush you!

THE SUPER IN SUPERGLUE

What is your mind focused upon in the midst of the temptation? When your thoughts are focused on King Me, your attention is on how this temptation is making *you* feel, what it's doing to you, and how hard—even impossible—it seems to fight it. Your motivation is all about getting away from it as fast as you can. "Get me outta here!"

> **Key Thought:** *The key to dealing with temptation and experiencing victory over sin begins with the focus of your mind—how and what you choose to think.*

God's command is clear: you are to "set your minds on things above, not on earthly things."[14] Think about glorifying God, not about satisfying King Me. The verb that Paul uses, "to set," involves making something firm and immovable—fixed or planted—almost as if it were set into cement or superglue.

Now, according to Colossians 3:2, your mind is to be firmly and immovably planted on *something specific*. It is not to wander away from that upon which it is set, no matter what enticing lure may come your way.

A set mind is an immovable mind. A set mind is fixed and focused on one thing. As Paul says, that something is "things above." You and I must make our minds firmly and permanently planted (superglued) on those things that are above.

The next question we need to zero in on is this: what are the "things above" that we should be thinking about? It is interesting to note that Paul uses the definite article here. I know it doesn't read well in English, but by using the definite article in the sentence, we can see what Paul is actually saying: "Set your minds on things *THE* above." Weird, right? Not really.

By writing it that way, he is making it clear that he's not referring to an ambiguous and undefined "above" that we can define however we want. If left to ourselves, the type of "things above" that we might we set our minds on would probably not be the things of God.[15]

By using the definite article, Paul helps us understand that there is only one singular thing our minds are to be set upon—Heaven, God's throne! Our minds are to be firmly, permanently fixed on the things of God.

Remember, what you think about directly affects what you say and what you do. Each and every thing you say and do should bring glory to God. This is why your mind must be firmly and permanently planted on God. If your mind is focused on King Me, everything you say and do will be for the purpose of making the King happy. When your mind is completely focused on God, all of your words and actions will be for His honor and glory.

Notice that Paul writes this verb, "set," in the present tense, active voice, and imperative mood. Here we go again!
- The *present tense* simply means that the action is being done now and never ends. It is continuous—ongoing, and always in the present. According to this verse, our minds are to always be firmly and movably planted on God—right now … right now … right now.
- However, this is not something that automatically happens for you or to you. The *active voice* means you are the one doing the action. You are the one who is continuously choosing to set your mind—firmly and immovably planting your thoughts—on God, not letting it wander. It is personal. No one else can do this for you; you must consistently do it yourself or it won't happen.
- Finally, this is a command. This is something that is your responsibility as a child of God. You MUST fix your mind firmly on the things of God. If you don't, you are sinning. Our minds must not ever wander away from the goal of glorifying God in everything we think, say, and do.

In 1 Chronicles 22:19 we read, "Set your mind and heart to seek the Lord your God." Are you firmly planting your heart—the very core of your being—on continuously seeking God?[16] Think about this for a moment. If your mind were firmly and immovably planted on the things of God, so that even the most tempting and enticing lure didn't draw you away, your life would be different. Your words and deeds would be different.

We *must* remove the "I" from LIFE! If you are going to glorify God in your daily life, you must first glorify him in your thought life. But how do we do that? We set our minds on God. We make every thought we think a thought that brings glory to our Heavenly Father.

GIVE IT SOME THOUGHT
❏ From this chapter, what primary truth stood out to you?

❏ What are you going to do in response to that truth? (Answer with "I am going to...")

Endnotes
1. 1 Timothy 4:2 (NIV '84)
2. 1 Thessalonians 5:19
3. Philippians 2:13
4. Jeremiah 29:11
5. Philippians 4:13
6. James 1:15
7. Hebrews 12:1
8. 1 John 2:21
9. Romans 7:23; Ephesians 6:10-17
10. Look at 1 Corinthians 10:13 in the KJV.
11. James 1:13
12. James 1:2 (NIV '84)
13. 1 Corinthians 10:13
14. Colossians 3:2 (NIV '84)
15. Psalm 10:4
16. 1 Chronicles 16:11; 28:9; compare with Matthew 6:33

> "Prepare your minds for action; be self-controlled; set your hope fully on the grace to be given you when Jesus Christ is revealed."
> 1 Peter 1:13

Eleven: The Favor of a Prepared Mind

For many Christians, Sunday is a day meant to focus all of our attention on God—a day of worship. We go to church, greet each other with a warm smile, sing worship songs as a congregation, open our Bibles and listen to the preacher deliver his well-prepared sermon, then cordially shake his hand on the way out the door. But did we really worship? Did we truly honor God from our hearts, or did we simply play "church"?

❏ Are you a one-day, only-on-Sunday Christian?

Unfortunately, many of us sit in the service and go through the motions while feeling numb and empty inside. The reason? We are in church for the wrong reason. You see, we should never go to church to worship God. Yes, we worship God while we're there, but we should never go because that's where we worship. Why not? We are to worship God everywhere and anywhere we are. When we walk into church on a Sunday morning, we are bringing our worship with us.

The real question here is, whom (or what) have you been worshipping during the week? It is impossible to walk in the doors of the church building and spiritually flip a switch from worshipping King Me all week long, to instantly worshipping God on Sunday. Whomever you are worshipping during the week is whom you will worship during the Sunday service.

To dethrone and depose King Me, we must be focused on God not just on Sundays but all during the week—not just when we're on the battlefield fighting temptation, but when we're in our La-Z-Boy enjoying some down time, as well.

ABOVE ALL ELSE
Have you ever stopped to consider what things around you, in your daily surroundings, impact and influence what and how you think?
❏ Write out Proverbs 4:23.

God says the most important thing here is to guard your heart. Let me repeat that slowly. *The—most—important—thing* is to guard your heart. Nothing is more important than this one thing. Guarding your heart must always take highest priority in your life.

OK, great. God says the most important thing I must do at all times is guard my heart. Why? Because it (my heart) is the wellspring of life ("out of it are the issues of life" KJV). That was a big help, eh? Actually, yes, it is. You see, "wellspring" (or "issues") refers to the primary source of something. It is the outpouring—the result.

The primary source of everything you say and do is your heart. The reason you say the things you say and do the things you do is because of what's in your heart. This is why it is of highest priority that you guard your heart. Guard your heart and you will guard your behavior, because what you think will become what you do.

The Favor of a Prepared Mind

What exactly is my "heart" and how do I guard it? In the Hebrew, "heart" is the word *leb* (pronounced Leh-bay), and it refers to the place where all of your thinking and decision-making occurs. It's the home of all your knowledge and understanding. It's your mind.

I know I'm repeating myself, but the primary source of everything you say and do is your mind. Therefore, Satan knows that if he can influence your thinking, he can impact your living. This is why it is of highest priority that you guard your mind. Guard what you think, and you will guard what you say and do.

❏ Name some ways you can guard your mind.

Just like the wells in ancient times could be tainted, affecting the community water source and thereby impacting people's health, so also can allowing sinful thoughts pollute your entire life.

If you are going to glorify God in all you say and do, everything you allow yourself to see and hear must also glorify God.

PREP TIME

Since your mind is the place where your behavior begins, it benefits you greatly to have a prepared mind.

> "Prepare your minds for action; be self-controlled; set your hope fully on the grace to be given you when Jesus Christ is revealed." (1 Peter 1:13, NIV '84)

Let's take a moment and think through this verse.

❏ When you are preparing for something, what are you doing? (e.g., preparing a meal or preparing for battle)

❏ According to 1 Peter 1:13, *what* are you supposed to prepare?

❏ According to 1 Peter 1:13, what are you supposed to prepare your mind *for*?

❏ What is the "action" you are to prepare for? (For example, see 2 Corinthians 11:3, 13-14; Matthew 24:4; Galatians 6:7. See also 1 Peter 5:8 and Titus 2:12.)

❏ How does one "prepare" his "mind" for "action?" (For example, see Colossians 4:2; 1 Thessalonians 5:17; Matthew 26:41; and 1 Peter 4:11; as well as Psalm 119:105 and Joshua 1:8.)

Eye to "I"

"The eye is the lamp of the body. So, if your eye is healthy, your whole body will be full of light, but if your eye is bad, your whole body will be full of darkness." (Matthew 6:22-23a)

Jesus says your eyes are like a lamp. Think of a "lamp" as a flashlight shining in the pitch-black night. Only, instead of that beam of light shining "out" from your eyes, it's actually shining inward to your soul. That "light" (what you see) is showing you how to live, where to go, and what to do.

Think of it this way: it would be rather silly of me to look to the left and yet walk to the right (while still looking left). I would eventually run into things and stub my toe, or something much worse. I'm going to walk where my eyes are looking. Why? Because what I see is going to influence what I do.

❑ What happens to your choices when the majority of the things you allow your eyes to see and ears to hear each day are sinful and ungodly?

Jesus is telling us that the things we see have a powerful influence on the things we do. If our eyes are good, if they are focused on things that will glorify God, then our actions and behavior will also glorify Him. However, if we allow our eyes to continuously view things that are ungodly, those things will wear us down and our lifestyle will eventually reflect that choice.

> **Key Thought:** *What the eye sees, the "I" does.*

Every moment of every day you are faced with choices about what you're going to permit yourself to see. With every choice there is a consequence.

Are you going to choose to see only those things that encourage you to live a godly life, or will you allow yourself to view the things that may tempt you to indulge in the lusts of the flesh? What you see influences what you think, which in turn directly impacts what you do. Let me repeat, what the eye sees greatly impacts what the "I" does.

Don't take my word for it, though.
> God "rescued Lot, a righteous man, who was distressed by the filthy lives of lawless men (for that righteous man, living among them day after day, was tormented in his righteous soul by the lawless deeds he *saw and heard*)." (2 Peter 2:7-8, NIV '84)

The wicked things that Lot chose to see day in and day out eventually impacted what he thought. His thoughts ultimately became wicked, which led him to make wicked, sinful, self-centered choices (read Genesis 19).

Daily, you make decisions about what you will watch, read, or even listen to. Most of the time you aren't conscious of those decisions, but you are making them. Paul challenges us to "be very careful, then, how you live—not as unwise but as wise, making the most of every opportunity, because the days are evil. Therefore do not be foolish, but understand what the Lord's will is."[2] Make the right choices.

Did you know that God has a will for you regarding what you should see and what you shouldn't? He has given you His Holy Word (the Bible) to shine a light on the path He wants you to walk.[3] So how do I know what I should look at and what I should not? Certainly, there are some things that are fairly obvious, like pornography—a definite no-no.[4] But what about those things that fit into those undefined, grey areas? Look to Scripture. Seriously—turn to the Word!

- "(God's) word is a lamp to my feet and a light to my path." (Psalm 119:105)
- "The unfolding of (God's) words gives light." (Psalm 119:130)
- God's "commandment is a lamp and (His) teaching a light." (Proverbs 6:23)
- "The commandment of the Lord is pure, enlightening the eyes." (Psalm 19:8)
- God's Word is "a lamp shining in a dark place." (2 Peter 1:19)

OCCUPIED TERRITORY

In Philippians 4:8 we are instructed to keep our *minds* occupied on things that are true, noble, right, pure, lovely, and admirable. Since what we see has a direct impact on what we think, it stands to reason that the things we see should also be true, noble, right, pure, lovely, and admirable. In the final analysis, anything you see that takes your love and focus away from God, from His Word, and from doing His will, doesn't belong in your life.

David warns us to turn our eyes away from looking at worthless things.[5] That's solid advice. In fact, he goes on to warn us to always

The Favor of a Prepared Mind

be careful about what we set before our eyes.[6] When we allow the wickedness of this world to enter our eyes and penetrate our minds, we run the high risk of our thought patterns becoming altered, which will eventually impact our behavior. What you think will affect what you do.

What do you watch on TV? What movies do you watch? What online games do you play? What magazines do you read?

What ungodly things are you exposing your mind to? What seed thoughts might the enemy be planting? Seeds grow. What crop will those seeds produce? Maybe not right away, but over time those seeds *will* sprout into weeds that *will* choke out the Word.[7]

If you do not guard your heart by being careful of what you allow your eyes to see, the deception of Satan will slowly creep in and warp your thinking, pulling you away from God. Never forget that bad company corrupts good morals. What kind of company are you allowing into your home and into your mind by way of your eyes? If you allow your eyes to see that which does not glorify God, you are allowing your mind to think on things that do not glorify God. Unless you guard your mind, it can result in a life that will not glorify God. Choices—consequences.

- ❏ Write out the following verses, then answer the question below.
    - ○ 1 Thessalonians 5:21-22

    - ○ Romans 16:17

    - ○ Mark 12:30

❏ How can the above verses be a guide to help you determine what you should see and what you should not?

If you haven't made the same commitment as David did, to "set before my eyes no vile thing,"[8] then I challenge you to commit to that right here and right now. Make the decision today to say, "My eyes are ever on the Lord, for only He will release my feet from the snare."[9]

HEAR YE, HEAR YE
Not only do the things you see have a powerful impact on what you do, so do the things you listen to. It is equally as important that you guard your mind from being attacked by the things you hear.
❏ Write out Proverbs 23:12.

We are to "apply" our ears to wisdom. God wants you to make an intentional, conscious effort to be aware of what you are hearing. Discipline yourself to permit only those things that glorify God to influence your thinking. Never allow yourself to hear "obscenity, foolish talk or coarse joking, which are out of place, but rather thanksgiving."[10]

Jesus warns us to "pay attention to what you hear."[11] That simple statement packs a very powerful punch. You see, the word "consider" refers to turning your thoughts to everything you are hearing, weighing every word carefully. Whether it's on the radio, TV, the movies, at school, work, talking sports with the guys, or even chatting with family—what you hear affects what you think, and what you think strongly influences what you do.

Every moment of every day you are personally responsible for what you hear. You are personally accountable to God for what you choose to listen to. Therefore, you must daily turn your thoughts to everything you're hearing, weighing every word, clinging only to those words that glorify God.

Remember Philippians 4:8? Our minds are to be thoroughly occupied with things that are true, noble, right, pure, lovely, and admirable.

For example, if a TV show or movie uses foul, vulgar language, or shows something sexual, turn it off or stand up and walk out of the theatre. Not after the fourth time, not after the third time; don't even allow it to go on past the first time. If it happened once, it's likely to happen again.

Paul exhorts us to "put them all away: anger, wrath, malice, slander, and obscene talk from your mouth."[12] Think about this: if I am not to be doing these things, then I shouldn't be exposing my mind to them!

GUARDING THE GATES
Your eyes and your ears are gateways into your mind. What you allow to enter through those gates will impact your effectiveness for Christ.

> **Key Thought:** *What we see and hear impacts what we think; what we think influences what we do!*

It is vital to your spiritual growth that you always set your focus on God. Never let it wander from Him, no matter what lure the enemy may use in an attempt to draw your attention away. Always be focused. Always be strong. Don't allow the worldly things you see each day to turn you away from following Christ.[13]

Remember, what we see influences what we think; and what we think impacts what we do. That is why ...
- We are to fix our eyes on Jesus (Hebrews 12:2);
- We are to fix God's words in our minds and in our hearts (Deuteronomy 11:18);

Removing the "I" from Life

- We are to fix our eyes, not on what is seen but what is unseen (2 Corinthians 4:18);
- We are to fix our thoughts on Christ (Hebrews 3:1).

What you allow yourself to think about—everything that goes on in your mind—matters to God. Scripture is quite clear on the issue. Set a guard around your mind, my friend. Lock it down tightly by being very careful about what you see and what you hear.

GIVE IT SOME THOUGHT

David asked God to "turn my eyes away from worthless things" (Psalm 119:37), and you are commanded to "set before [your] eyes no vile thing" (Psalm 101:3).

Let's consider the "worthless things" and "vile things" you need to turn your eyes away from. Getting down to the nitty-gritty, answer the following questions honestly:

❏ What TV shows and movies do you watch? Make a specific list using the table below.

TV Show/Movie	Purpose in watching	Time spent

- ✓ Look carefully at that list and circle the ones that glorify God.
- ✓ How is each show helping you *learn* to glorify God?
- ✓ What is your primary purpose in watching each show?
- ✓ How much time each day do you spend watching TV / movies?
- ✓ How do you respond when a TV show or movie uses foul language or implies (directly or indirectly) something sexual? Why?
- ✓ How do you respond when an activity that is inappropriate takes place? Why?

❏ What websites do you frequent? Again, be specific, using the table below.

Website	Purpose in visiting/viewing	Time spent

- ✓ Look carefully at that list and circle the ones that glorify God.
- ✓ How is each website helping you learn to glorify God?
- ✓ What is your primary purpose for visiting each website?
- ✓ How much time each day do you spend visiting each website?
- ✓ How do you respond when an inappropriate image or content appears? Why?

❏ What books or magazines do you read? Be specific, using the table below.

Book / Magazine	Purpose in reading	Time spent

- ✓ Look carefully at that list and circle the ones that help you grow in your walk with God
- ✓ How is each book/magazine helping you learn to glorify God?
- ✓ What is your primary purpose for reading each book / magazine?
- ✓ How much time each day do you spend reading each book / magazine?

❑ What video games do you play? Be specific, using the table below.

Game	Purpose in playing	Time spent

- ✓ Look carefully at that list and circle the ones that glorify God.
- ✓ How is that game helping you learn to glorify God?
- ✓ What is your primary purpose in playing each game?
- ✓ How much time do you spend each day playing each game?

❏ How much time to you invest each day reading & studying the Bible?

Endnotes
1. Genesis 26:15
2. Ephesians 5:15-17 (NIV '84)
3. Psalm 119:105; compare with Psalm 19:8; 43:3; Proverbs 6:23
4. Matthew 5:28
5. Psalm 119:37
6. Psalm 101:2-3
7. Matthew 13:22
8. Psalm 101:3
9. Psalm 25:15
10. Ephesians 5:4 (NIV '84)
11. Mark 4:24
12. Colossians 3:8
13. Joshua 1:7, Deuteronomy 28:14; Joshua 23:6

> "But I say, walk by the Spirit, and you will not gratify the desires of the flesh."
> Galatians 5:16

Twelve: The Spirit Walk

As long as you live here on planet Earth you are going to daily experience the epic battle between King Me and King Jesus—there's just no way to avoid it.[1] The great news is that although you will always struggle against your selfish desires, you do not have to give in to them.[2]

Look at God's promise in Galatians 5:16. "Walk by the Spirit, and you will not gratify the desires of the flesh."
- ❏ What does it mean to *walk* (live) by the Spirit?

The word Paul uses for "walk" refers to regulating or conducting your life according to a specific purpose or guide. There is a specific set of standards and guidelines that you are to always follow.
- ❏ What are the standards and guidelines you are to follow, and where do you find them?

Paul's instruction is to take charge of your life, living in such a way that you are constantly making decisions and adjustments to your

daily walk, so that you are living according to the leading of the Holy Spirit.
- ❏ Write out Romans 8:14.

- ❏ Write out John 6:13.

How does the Holy Spirit lead you? How do you know what guidelines and standards you should follow? He uses God's truth—the Scripture—to guide you.³ As you read God's Word, studying it, memorizing it, and meditating on it, the Holy Spirit will bring to your remembrance what God says you should do, every time you face a temptation and need to make a decision.

We are to daily walk by the Spirit. "Walk by the Spirit" is a very interesting command. Paul wrote it in the present tense, active voice, and imperative mood. Do you remember what that means?
- ❏ By using the *present tense*, Paul is telling us that every moment of every day you need to regulate your life; conducting yourself—making all your decisions, choices, and actions—according to the leading of the Holy Spirit. As He reveals God's truth to you, showing you things you need to either do or stop doing, you choose to *immediately yield* (present tense) your life to Him and put that truth into action in your life right now...right now...right now. This is walking by the Spirit.
- ❏ By using the *active voice*, Paul is saying that this is something *you* have to do. No one else can do it for you. It is personal. If you don't do it, it won't get done. Living every moment of every day under the direction of the Holy Spirit is something that only you can do. Only you can hear the promptings of the Holy Spirit as He guides you into God's truth. Only you

can make the moment-by-moment decisions to yield to His will and apply God's truth immediately to your life.
- ❏ This isn't an option. It's a command (*imperative mood*)! We are commanded by God to conduct our everyday living according to the leading of the Holy Spirit. When I choose not to obey, I am sinning.

Notice also that the verb "walk by" indicates forward movement. When you're walking, you're moving. You are going from point A to point B; from where you are right now to where you ought to be. We often call this "spiritual growth."

You see, step by step the Holy Spirit directs you, moving you from where you are to where God wants you to be. The Holy Spirit is your guide. Only as you choose to submit your life to the Spirit's control will you move forward—growing spiritually.
- ❏ Where are you right now in your spiritual walk, and where does God want you to be?

The victorious Christian life is a life lived under the direction of, and through the power of, the Holy Spirit. The Spirit of God is not some force or power for you to use. He is a Person of the Godhead to whom you are to yield, and to *let Him use you*!

> **Key Thought:** *Holy living doesn't come from the things you do for God, but from what He does through you as you walk by the Holy Spirit.*

Never forget the total necessity of dethroning and deposing King Me. If you are going to glorify God in your everyday living, He must first be glorified in your every-moment thinking. Paul commands each of us to "clothe yourselves with the Lord Jesus Christ, and do not think about how to gratify the desires of the (flesh)."[4] What you think becomes what you do. When King Me is sitting on the throne of your heart, everything you think, say, and do will be for the benefit of King Me.

OH MERCY!
❑ Write out Romans 12:1.

Now take a moment and read what you just wrote. Paul isn't saying, "Wow. It would be awesome if you would offer your body daily to God. You really ought to think about doing that." No, he says, "I urge you!" Paul means, "I am calling you to my side to lovingly admonish you. This is of utmost importance. Make the choice to offer your bodies every moment to God as a living sacrifice."

Why is this so important to Paul? Why should this be so important to us? It's because of God's great mercy. "Mercy" is a word that refers to compassion and pity. It has been said that His mercy is "God *not* giving to us what we deserve." Think about that. "He saved us, not because of righteous things we had done, but because of His mercy."[5]

Peter said, "According to (God's) great mercy, he has caused us to be born again to a living hope through the resurrection of Jesus Christ from the dead."[6] We deserve death, not life.[7] Yet God, in His great compassion and pity (mercy), has declared that anyone who believes on His Son will not receive the death they deserve, but will have eternal life![8] Why? Because in God's grace He took our place.
- God's mercy is great.[9]
- He shows us His great mercy because of His great love.[10]
- It is because of God's mercy that He does not abandon us.[11]
- His mercy enables us to come boldly into His presence without fear.[12]
- God has promised His mercy to those who reject sinful thinking, turn to Him, and confess and renounce their sin.[13]
- God delights in showing us His mercy.[14]

So, "in view of God's mercy," because of the fact that God has not given to you what you deserve, Paul urges you to offer your body to God. His call is for every believer to remove the "I" from LIFE and dedicate every aspect of themselves without reservation to the Lord.

Let me emphasize the fact that this exhortation is given only to the born-again believer. Paul calls us "brothers." You see, "The man without the Spirit does not accept the things that come from the Spirit of God, for they are foolishness to him, and he cannot understand them, because they are spiritually discerned."[15]

Only the born-again believer can present his body as a living sacrifice to God, because only the Christian can come before God with such an offering. The unsaved haven't recognized their need, and accepted God's gracious gift of washing and renewing by the Word and the Spirit. They are not presentable before God; therefore, they cannot serve or worship God in any way that will be acceptable to Him.

SWEET SURRENDER

Focus for a moment on the fact that Paul says you are to "offer" your body to God. The word "offer" is a term that was used to describe the way a priest places an offering on the altar for the purpose of surrendering or yielding it up to God—willingly putting it to death, giving up ownership.

As a Christian, "you also, like living stones, are being built into a spiritual house to be a *holy priesthood, offering spiritual sacrifices* acceptable to God through Jesus Christ."[16] You are considered by God to be a "priest" and, as such, you are to offer—to daily yield—your body to God. You are called to make your body available for God to use, every moment of every day, in any way He desires. This is your priestly act of worship.

❏ Why present our *bodies* as a sacrifice to God?

Removing the "I" from Life

Imagine you are driving down the road in a vehicle that desperately needs its wheels aligned. Every time you let go of the wheel, the vehicle naturally veers to the left, placing you at high risk for a serious accident. As a result, you have to constantly fight with the steering wheel just to keep the car on your side of the road.

This is much the same with your body. Think of it as the "car" God created for you in which to navigate through life. Because of sin, your "car" is permanently out of alignment. Left to itself, the natural bent of your body is to sin.

To prevent that from happening, you must choose to daily grab hold of the "wheel" and fight with it to keep it going in the correct direction. You must daily—moment-by-moment—place your body on the altar, yielding it completely to the will of the Spirit to do service for God instead of serving self.

If you allow it, your body can, and will, frustrate the desires of your new nature to please God.[17] Your body is still the beachhead of sin. It is permanently out of alignment; and if left to its own, it will steer you wrong every time.

As long as you are alive here on earth, your new holy nature will reside in a damaged, sinful body of flesh that can readily give in to sinful thoughts and longings. There is a constant battle going on between King Me and King Jesus.[18] This is why you are to continually present your body to God as a living sacrifice.

❏ Write out Romans 6:12.

Notice that Paul uses the word "not" in this verse. It is an absolute negation. He is telling us that in no way or at any time is this ever to happen. Sin must *never* be allowed to reign in your body—not even for a moment.

Also notice in this verse that the words "let reign" refer to exercising kingly power over someone. If you do not submit control of your body to God, sin will walk all over you. Your flesh desires to be king, reigning over your new nature—dictating what you will and will not do. If you allow sin to rule in your body, you will end up obeying it instead of God. Sin desires to have you, but you must rule over it.[19] This is why you must dethrone and depose King Me—removing the "I" from LIFE.

Think for a moment about the word "obey" in Romans 6:12 above. To obey is to listen to the command of another and do what you have been told.

> **Key Thought:** *When you obey your flesh, you are choosing to deny God's truth in favor of the desires of your sinful body.*

That leads us to Paul's use of the word "desires" (lusts). It refers to cravings and longings for that which is forbidden—the things you, as a child of God, should not have or do. Jesus says, "No one can serve two masters, for either he will hate the one and love the other, or he will be devoted to the one and despise the other. You cannot serve God and *(fill in the blank with your sin)*."[20]

THE CHOICE IS YOURS

You are faced with a choice daily. God's command is that you make the decision to never let sin reign, otherwise you will end up obeying its evil desires and disobeying God. The way you make that choice is to daily offer your body as a living sacrifice. Choose to yield to God moment-by-moment, day-by-day.

> "Don't you know that when you offer yourselves to someone to obey him as slaves, you are slaves to the one whom you obey—whether you are slaves to sin, which leads to death, or to obedience, which leads to righteousness?" (Romans 6:16 NIV '84)

You make choices throughout each day that reveal who you are yielding to in obedience.

Removing the "I" from Life

> **Key Thought:** *Do you let sin reign so that you obey its desires, or do you say no to ungodliness, and choose to live by the Spirit in obedience to God?*

The bottom line is that "whoever keeps his commandments abides in God, and God in in him. And by this we know that he abides in us, by the Spirit whom he has given us."[21] Love for God is demonstrated when you "obey His commands. And His commands are not burdensome."[22]

MY BODY PARTS

You are dependent upon your body for more than just living, breathing, and moving. It is through the use of your body that you either glorify God or magnify self. This is why it's so vital that you learn how to yield to the Spirit's control of your body, and so that you can offer it daily as a sacrifice to God.

> **Key Thought:** *You cannot glorify God in your daily life apart from your body.*

We know that our aim as Christians is to glorify God in everything we say and do.[23] But consider this carefully:
- ❏ What are some ways you can use your body to glorify God?

Peter says you are to "live such good lives among the pagans that, though they accuse you of doing wrong, they may see your *good deeds* and glorify God."[24] How can the unsaved see your good deeds apart from your body? They can't.

Jesus admonishes you to "let your light shine before others, so that they may *see your good works* and give glory to your Father who is in heaven."[25] The activities you choose to do with your body are what people see. It is when you yield to God in your daily actions, that you bear much fruit and show yourself to be His disciple.[26]

When you choose to let the flesh rule in your life, your attitudes and actions will reveal it, because "the works of the flesh are evident: sexual immorality, impurity, sensuality, idolatry, sorcery, enmity, strife, jealousy, fits of anger, rivalries, dissensions, divisions, envy, drunkenness, orgies, and things like these."[27] Look carefully at that list. There is not a single thing there that glorifies God. There is not one item in that list that demonstrates the power of God to a lost world around you. Your life reflects your choices.

> **Key Thought:** *When you choose to please the sinful desires of your flesh, God promises you will reap destruction.*[28]

However, when you choose to walk by the Spirit, yielding control of your life over to Him, it will be just as obvious because "the fruit of the Spirit is love, joy, peace, patience, kindness, goodness, faithfulness, gentleness, self-control."[29] Now, look at *that* list. Every one of those things brings honor and glory to God. Why? Because it's the fruit of *His* Spirit—not yours.

None of those things are of your own doing. They are the fruit *of* (or belonging to) the Holy Spirit. When those things are evident in your life, it's not because you have produced the right kind of love or have generated the correct amount of patience or kindness. When there is love, joy, peace, patience, kindness, goodness, faithfulness, gentleness, and self-control evident in your life, it is solely because you have fully yielded to the Holy Spirit and *His* fruit is being seen through your daily living.

❑   Write out Romans 6:13.

You cannot prevent sin from attempting to exert control over your body. But, through Christ, you are able to keep sin from *ruling* in your body by making a continuous, conscious choice to offer yourself entirely to God, which includes every part of your body.

Praise the Lord, there is a day coming when you will no longer need to concern yourself with this. As a born-again believer, your "citizenship is in heaven, and from it we await a Savior, the Lord Jesus Christ, who will transform our lowly body to be like his glorious body."[30]

I can't wait for that day! I hate the way my body is always working against me. Sometimes the temptations I experience, and the deep cravings for sinful pleasures they present, are almost overwhelming. I understand what Paul meant when he said, "We ourselves who have the firstfruits of the Spirit, groan inwardly as we wait eagerly for adoption as sons, the redemption of our bodies."[31]

What is the *inward groaning* Paul is talking about? It is the new nature crying out for deliverance from our sinful bodies, so that we can live the life we were created for—glorifying Him.

Until that time, do not lose sight of the fact that right now your body is the "temple of the Holy Spirit within you, whom you have from God, you are not your own."[32] Through God's divine power[33] you are able to say no to the reign of sin in your body. It is by the Spirit that you are able to "put to death the deeds of the body."[34]

> **Key Thought:** *Paul says your body is meant for the Lord, and the Lord for your body.[35] Since your body already belongs to God, offering it to Him as a living sacrifice is a reasonable and spiritual act of worship.*

COUNTING WITH A BEAT

"We know that our old self was crucified with him in order that the body of sin might be brought to nothing, so that we would no longer be enslaved to sin. For one who has died has been set free from sin...So you also must consider yourselves dead to sin and alive to God in Christ Jesus. Let not sin therefore reign in your mortal body, to make you obey its passions. Do not present your members to sin as instruments for unrighteousness, but present yourselves to God as those who have been brought from death to life, and your members to God as instruments for righteousness. For sin will have no dominion over you, since you are not under law but under grace." (Romans 6:6-7, 11-14)

I want you to notice that Paul said that the "old self was crucified" with Christ. Your old nature is dead and gone, my friend. Therefore, the influence of sin no longer has dominion over you. Because of Christ's finished work on Calvary you have been freed from sin! Since this is God's absolute truth, you need to *count* yourselves dead to sin. Take it to the bank of Heaven as fact. God said it, and that settles it.

Now think about this: although sin can still reign in your body, it cannot reign in your new nature. Why is that so significant? Your old nature is dead and gone, never to come back again. Sin does not and cannot reign there because you have within you a new, holy nature that is incapable of sinning (for a full treatise on this topic, see Chapters 4 and 5 of my book *Extreme Mind Makeover: How to Transform Sinful Thoughts and Habits into God-Pleasing Patterns*, Overboard Ministries, 2012). Therefore, the only place sin can reside is in your body—in your humanness—and God commands you to not let that sin have free rein in your life. Don't let your body have *any* kingly authority over you.

Through your new nature, God has given you the ability not to sin. Don't forget—through the power of the Holy Spirit, your body can be controlled.[36] This is why I emphasize so strongly that you don't have to sin.

> Key Thought: *You sin because you choose to; and you choose to because it brings temporary, self-satisfying pleasure. You do what you do because in your heart you want what you want.*

> "The grace of God that brings salvation has appeared to all men. It teaches us to say 'No' to ungodliness and worldly passions, and to live self-controlled, upright and godly lives in this present age." (Titus 2:11-12 NIV '84)

Saying "no" to ungodliness and worldly passions and living a self-controlled, godly life is a daily decision you have to make—not just when you wake up in the morning, but all the time.

In every instance where you are faced with a temptation, you are also faced with a decision. Do I give in this time, or do I continue to stand firm and fight it?[37] Do I yield to the Spirit and glorify God, or focus on myself? You are constantly using your mind throughout the day to make decisions. This is why it is vital that you discipline your mind to say "no" to the flesh and "yes" to the Holy Spirit.

RUN THE RACE — RUN HARD

Let's take a closer look at what Paul says in 1 Corinthians 9:24-27.

> "Do you not know that in a race all the runners run, but only one receives the prize? So run that you may obtain it. Every athlete exercises self-control in all things. They do it to receive a perishable wreath, but we an imperishable. So I do not run aimlessly; I do not box as one beating the air. But I discipline my body and keep it under control, lest after preaching to others I myself should be disqualified."

The first thing I want you to notice is that Paul likens the Christian life to that of a long-distance runner. Now, I'm not much of a runner (truth be told, I don't run at all), but I do know that in order to run the distance you have to be in shape.

In verse 25, Paul says, "Every athlete exercises self-control in all things." That runner has to train himself in such a way that he is able to control the self-centered longings and desires of the flesh so that he can accomplish his ultimate goal. If he doesn't, he runs the high risk that those desires are going to keep him from receiving his prize.

That kind of control involves denying fleshly desires, ignoring the cries of his body for rest, relaxation, and certain pleasures. The one who trains for the run must constantly push and exert his body, taking it to the limit and beyond—all for the purpose of winning the prize at the end of the race. He knows that if he gives in and yields to the desires of his body, he will not be able to finish the course and win the race.

As a Christian, you should also deny your fleshly desires. You should ignore the cries of your body for sinful pleasures. Giving in may be enjoyable for the moment, but the long-term ramifications aren't worth it. You should live each day with the understanding that if you choose to yield to the sinful desires of your body, you will compromise your ability to run the race, and you will not be able to fulfill your life's purpose.

Paul goes on to say, "They do it to receive a perishable wreath, but we an imperishable." The athlete running in a race knows there is the risk that she will not win. So, she pushes herself beyond her limits so that she might win the prize at the end of the race.

The exciting thing about the race Christians are running is that every Christian who applies himself to careful training, submitting to God's Spirit in his inner man, will win! This is why Paul counsels us to run in such a way as to obtain the prize.

We aren't running for a laurel wreath that will die, or for fame that will fade with time. We are running to receive "an imperishable wreath" (a crown that will last forever). Paul calls it a "crown of righteousness, which the Lord, the righteous judge, will award to me on that day, and not only to me but also to all who have loved his appearing."[38] This is a grand and glorious prize "that is imperishable, undefiled, and unfading, kept in heaven for you."[39]
- ❏ Write out Hebrews 12:1.

Running this race isn't easy. It requires perseverance through the rough times, always seeking the joy of the Lord as our strength. It means that we endure the pain of trials and testing, pushing through it by the power of the Spirit. The only way we can run like this is to go into strict training, just like athletes.

Nope, Can't Do That

When athletes are preparing for the main event, they place specific restrictions upon themselves. They are careful about their diet, sleep, exercise, and other aspects of their lives. They set up daily routines and do not deviate from them. This isn't something that comes naturally for them; they submit themselves to the conditions that will help them achieve their goals.

It is no different for you and me, dear friend. If you expect to grow and excel in your spiritual life, you must place specific restrictions upon yourself—and then choose to keep them. You need to be careful about your spiritual diet. What are you allowing to enter your mind through the things you see and hear? Train yourself to be godly.[40]

❏ What are the restrictions you need to put into place so that you can run your spiritual race?

Paul also says we should not live our Christian life without a purpose or goal in mind. In verse 26 he says, "I do not run like a man running aimlessly; I do not fight like a man beating the air." The person who runs with a purpose is looking straight ahead to his goal. All of his attention is focused on the finish line. We read in the book of Hebrews that we are to "lay aside every weight, and the sin which clings so closely, and let us run with endurance the race that is set before us, looking to Jesus, the founder and perfecter of our faith."[41]

The person who runs with a purpose doesn't give up. The person who runs with intent pushes on no matter what. Paul expressed it this way: "I press on toward the goal for the prize of the upward call of God in Christ Jesus."[42] To "press on" means to run swiftly in order to catch the thing you are pursuing. Don't quit. Don't give up.

❏ When do you feel most tempted to give up, and why?

STEPPING INTO THE RING

Paul moves his illustration to that of a boxer who is shadow boxing.[43] Although shadow boxing can help a boxer warm up his muscles and settle into a rhythm, it does not constitute real boxing. He is hitting the air, not fighting his adversary. Shadow boxing is simply a means of getting ready for the main event. In real boxing, there is a purpose to each blow.

Paul's point is this: if all you ever do is shadow box spiritually, if all you do is put on a show for others, you will not know genuine spiritual victory. You need to actually step into the ring and strike precise blows against your enemy—which, in this case, is your sinful flesh.

This leads us to verse 27, where Paul says, "No, I beat my body and make it my slave." Why? Because "in me, that is, in my flesh dwells no good thing."[44] If you do not submit control of your body to the Holy Spirit, it will lead you down the path of sin every time (just like that car with its wheels out of alignment). You cannot—you must not—let your body's sinful tendencies dictate to you what you will and will not do. It must never exercise kingly authority over you.

God's will is that you be sanctified (living a life that is set apart for Him), and He instructs you to learn how to control your body in a way that is holy and honorable.[45] When you give in to the desires of your flesh, you won't be yielding to the desires of the Holy Spirit and Christ won't be exalted in your body through those actions.

❏ Write out 1 Corinthians 6:19-20.

Every Christian is to live a life worthy of the calling we have received.[46] We are commanded to "cleanse ourselves from every defilement of body and spirit, bringing holiness to completion in the fear of God."[47] This means we *must* take control of our bodies.

Looking again at 1 Corinthians 9:27, we see that Paul uses a very strong term. He says he "beats" his body. It literally means "to turn black and blue." Now wait a minute; does this mean we should take a whip or bat and literally beat ourselves? Is Paul advocating self-flagellation? Most emphatically not! This concept means you are to treat your body with severity, subjecting it to stern and rigid discipline, leaving no room for error.

You are to deny your body the sinful pleasures it craves. You are to be stern and rigid in the discipline of your body. No matter how much your flesh cries out for satisfaction and fulfillment, if what it craves does not glorify God, you must deny what it wants. That will often involve great difficulty and even, sometimes, pain. This is why Paul uses the phrase "beat my body."

A CAN-DO ATTITUDE
❑ Write out Romans 8:11.

It is possible to just say "no" to the desires of the flesh.[48] You have the power of the One who raised Christ from the dead living within you! Think about that. The very same power that raised the dead is enabling you to deny the sinful desires of the flesh and make it do that which will glorify God.

Again, it's important to understand that you do not have to sin. You have a choice. Every time you sin, you have willingly chosen its short-term pleasures (along with the consequences) over the eternal joys of living for God. When you make that choice—when you choose to sin—you are offering, willingly handing over, your body to sin instead of choosing to be a "living sacrifice."[49]

It's hard to be the master of your body, isn't it? Paul worded it so well in Romans 7 when he said, "I find it to be a law that when I want to do right, evil lies close at hand. For I delight in the law of God, in my inner being, but I see in my members another law waging war against the law of my mind and making me captive to the law of sin that dwells in my members."[50]

❏ Write out Galatians 2:20.

I want you to notice Paul's reference to the "life I now live in the flesh." This is huge. That life you live *in the body*, you are to live by faith! Why is that so important? Remember Paul's question in Romans 7:24? "Who will deliver me from this body of death?" His answer was, "Thanks be to God through Jesus Christ our Lord!"[51] Only God can give you victory over sinful flesh.

You are not in this fight alone! You don't have to fight against King Me without God's help. The question you need to ask yourself is this:

❏ Do I believe that God can and will help me achieve victory over the flesh?

❏ Do I really want Him to?

Too often we yearn for the Wizard of the Word (God) to just wave His magic wand and make our struggles with the flesh go away, making everything suddenly and miraculously better. Although God could do that, it's not usually how He accomplishes His purposes.

Removing the "I" from Life

You must never forget that your mind plays a crucial role in living a life that glorifies God. To glorify God in your everyday living, you must first glorify Him in your every-moment thinking. This is why you are not to even think about how to gratify the desires of the flesh.[52] If you do, you're like a fish playing with a deadly lure.[53]

When you choose to walk by the Spirit, you will not gratify the desires of the flesh.[54]

> **Key Thought:** *If you want to gain spiritual victory over King Me, you need to daily make the decision to say "no" to the flesh and "yes" to the Holy Spirit.*

Walk by the Spirit. Live by the Spirit. That is when you will dethrone and depose King Me. That is when you will experience lasting victory!

GIVE IT SOME THOUGHT

- ❏ How will walking by the Spirit (Galatians 5:16) keep you from gratifying the desires of King Me?

- ❏ How often each day should you walk by the Spirit? How do you plan to accomplish that? Be specific.

- ❏ If you were to quit trying to be godly, and instead put your focus completely on yielding to the Holy Spirit, what would be different in your life?

❏ Have you ever felt tired of fighting the battle with sin? Why does that happen?

Endnotes
1. Romans 7:15-25
2. 1 Corinthians 10:13
3. John 16:13
4. Romans 13:14 (NIV '84)
5. Titus 3:5 (NIV '84)
6. 1 Peter 1:3 (addition mine)
7. Romans 3:23
8. 1 Timothy 1:16
9. 2 Samuel 24:14; 1 Chronicles 21:13
10. Nehemiah 13:22; Psalm 25:6; Ephesians 2:4
11. Nehemiah 9:31
12. Psalm 5:7; Hebrews 4:16
13. Proverbs 28:13; Isaiah 55:7
14. Micah 7:18
15. 1 Corinthians 2:14 (NIV '84)
16. 1 Peter 2:5 (NIV '84, emphasis mine)
17. Romans 7:18
18. Galatians 5:17
19. Genesis 4:7
20. Matthew 6:24 (addition mine)
21. 1 John 3:24
22. 1 John 5:3 (NIV '84)
23. 1 Corinthians 10:31; Colossians 3:17
24. 1 Peter 2:12 (NIV '84)
25. Matthew 5:16 (emphasis mine)
26. John 15:8
27. Galatians 5:19-21
28. Galatians 6:8
29. Galatians 5:22-23

30. Philippians 3:20-21
31. Romans 8:23
32. 1 Corinthians 6:19
33. 2 Peter 1:3
34. Romans 8:13
35. 1 Corinthians 6:13
36. 1 Corinthians 9:27
37. James 4:7
38. 2 Timothy 4:8
39. 1 Peter 1:4
40. 1 Timothy 4:7
41. Hebrews 12:1-2
42. Philippians 3:14
43. 1 Corinthians 9:26
44. Romans 7:18 (NIV '84)
45. 1 Thessalonians 4:3-4
46. Ephesians 4:1
47. 2 Corinthians 7:1
48. Titus 2:12
49. Romans 12:1
50. Romans 7:21-23
51. Romans 7:25
52. Romans 13:14 (NIV '84)
53. James 1:14-15
54. Galatians 5:16

About the Author

Steve Etner is a national men's speaker. Through the Pure Man Ministry, Steve coaches men across the globe, sharing God's truth in such a way as to help guys become men of godliness, purity and integrity. Steve has authored *Extreme Mind Makeover: How to transform thoughts and habits into God-pleasing patterns*, *The Pure Man's Devotional Guide: A biblical toolbox for purity,* and *"Are You A Super Man? Becoming God's Man of Steel.* He and his wife, Heather, live in Granger, Indiana.

Acknowledgement

*"The pleasantness of one's friend springs
from his earnest counsel."*
Proverbs 27:9b

Thank you, Joe Castaneda. Your friendship, and your belief in me, has been an encouragement throughout the writing of each of my books. You took a risk in becoming my publisher; I have reaped the rewards tenfold in finding an amazing brother in Christ!

About Overboard Ministries

Overboard Books is the publishing arm of Overboard Ministries, whose mission is based on Matthew 14. In that chapter we find the familiar story of Jesus walking on water while His disciples were in a boat. It was the middle of the night, the water was choppy and Jesus freaked out His followers who thought He was a ghost. When they realized it was Him, Peter asked to come out to Him on the water, and he actually walked on top of the water like Jesus.

But what truly captivates me is the thought of the other eleven disciples who remained in the boat. I've often wondered how many of them questioned that move in the years to come? How many of them wished they hadn't stayed in the boat but had instead gone overboard with Peter? Overboard Ministries aims to help Christians get out of the boat and live life out on the water with Christ. We hope and pray that each book published by Overboard Ministries will stir believers to jump overboard and live life all-out for God, full of joy and free from the regret of "I wish I had…"

What we do
Overboard Ministries emerged in the Spring of 2011 as an umbrella ministry for several concepts my wife and I were developing. One of those concepts was a book ministry that would help other Christian authors get published. I experienced a lot of frustration while passing my first manuscript around. I kept getting rejection letters that were kindly written, but each echoed the same sentiment: "We love this book. If you were already a published author, we would love to publish it." They were nice letters, but that didn't make the rejection any easier or the logic less frustrating.

Out of that came the audacious idea to start our own "publishing company." I put that in quotes because I want people to know a couple of things. First of all, we're not a traditional publishing company like most people envision when they hear the name. We don't have a printing press in our garage, and we don't have a marketing team. Basically, we're a middle-man who absorbs most of the cost of publishing in order to help you get published, while making sure the majority of profits end up in your pocket, not ours.

Our desire is to keep costs to a bare minimum for each author. (As of this writing, there is only a minimal contract fee when your manuscript is accepted.) We provide resources and ideas to help authors work on marketing, while also providing the editor and graphic design artist at our expense. We subcontract out the printing, which speeds up the time it takes to move from final draft to bound book. Since we don't have much overhead we can keep our expenses low, allowing seasoned authors, or first-time authors like me, the opportunity to profit from their writing.

Contact us
If you are interested in other books or learning about other authors from Overboard Books, please visit our website at www.overboardministries.com and click on the "Store" link. If you are an author interested in publishing with us, please visit our site and check out the "Authors" tab. There you will find a wealth of information that will help you understand the publishing process and how we might be a good fit for you. If we're not a fit for you, we'll gladly share anything we've learned that might be helpful to you as you pursue publishing through other means.

Thank you
Thanks for supporting our work and ministry. If you believe this book was helpful to you, tell someone about it! Or better yet, buy them a copy of their own! We completely depend on word-of-mouth grassroots marketing to help spread the word about Overboard Ministries and its publications. Please share our website with others and encourage them to purchase the materials that will help them live "overboard" lives for Christ.

May God bless you as you grab the side of boat, take a deep breath… and jump onto the sea!

Joe Castañeda
Founder, Overboard Ministries

Made in the USA
Columbia, SC
21 December 2018